ONE
FAMILY
UNDER
GOD

THE LIFE UNDER GOD SERIES

ONE
FAMILY
UNDER
GOD

Preserving the Home as God Intended

TONY EVANS

MOODY PUBLISHERS
CHICAGO

Scripture quotations are taken from the *New American Standard Bible®*, Copyright © 1960, 1962, 1963, 1968, 1971, 1972, 1973, 1975, 1977, 1995 by The Lockman Foundation. Used by permission. (www.Lockman.org)

Scripture quotations marked KJV are taken from the King James Version.

Scripture quotations marked THE MESSAGE are from *The Message,* copyright © by Eugene H. Peterson 1993, 1994, 1995. Used by permission of NavPress Publishing Group.

Emphasis in Scripture is the author's.

Edited by Bailey Utecht
Interior design: Erik Peterson
Cover design: Smartt Guys design
Cover image: Fotosearch / Superstock

ISBN: 978-0-8024-1141-9

We hope you enjoy this book from Moody Publishers. Our goal is to provide high-quality, thought-provoking books and products that connect truth to your real needs and challenges. For more information on other books and products written and produced from a biblical perspective, go to www.moodypublishers.com or write to:

Moody Publishers
820 N. LaSalle Boulevard
Chicago, IL 60610

1 3 5 7 9 10 8 6 4 2

Printed in the United States of America

CONTENTS

CHAPTER ONE

THE FOUNDATION CRISIS

The saga of a nation is the saga of its families written large. If we are to reverse the course that we are heading in as a society, it must start with the rebuilding of our families.

In the book of Nehemiah, God's chosen people are going through national, cultural, and family crises. The society is in disrepair, wasting away. Their captors have torn down Jerusalem's defensive walls, and the people of Israel have been living in exile for 150 years.

During this critical time, God raised up two men who were willing to lead their people from physical ruin. God put a fire in Ezra's and Nehemiah's hearts to lead His chosen people and to urge them to fight for their families. Nehemiah and Ezra understood that in order to repair a broken society, you must not only rebuild the walls, you must rebuild the people.

You must remind them about the importance of family. Lasting change must occur in individual hearts and in homes.

At the beginning of Nehemiah's story, Ezra had already been preaching in Jerusalem for fourteen years. He was sowing seeds into people's hearts, telling them to listen, learn, and believe in God. In the midst of this spiritual environment, Ezra had created hope for social change. The ground had been softened with spiritual truth, admonishing the people to base their lives on the standard of truth, which would then translate into the political and social arena.

God's Word made the way for social change, family renewal and cultural transformation. When the fertile ground was ready, God brought Nehemiah in.

Fast-forward just a bit and we see that Nehemiah rebuilt the city's entire infrastructure in a mere fifty-two days. In less than two months, Nehemiah solidified the foundation of not only the families but of a nation whose stature had crumbled just assuredly as Jerusalem's walls under 150 years of total confusion and disrepute. Nehemiah dealt with the physical needs of this people, repairing the fissures and building upon a firm and solid foundation.

But in the midst of this rebuilding effort, opposition rose up against them. As I say it, there were haters in the house. There were people who didn't want to see the society turn back to God, wholeness, and wholesomeness. We read in Nehemiah,

Now it came about that when Sanballat heard that we were rebuilding the wall, he became furious and very angry and mocked the Jews. . . . Now when Sanballat, Tobiah, the Arabs, the Ammonites and the Ashdodites heard that the repair of the walls of Jerusalem went on, and that the breaches began to be closed, they were very angry. All of them conspired together to come and fight against Jerusalem and to cause a disturbance in it. (Nehemiah 4:1, 7–8)

The opposition had determined that they were not going to allow this nation to return back to God's intended purposes. They did not want to see society ordered as God had decreed and established, so they began to devise a plan in order to make the Israelites fail.

Friend, Satan has a plan against the house of God today as well. As our nation continues to steer away further from God's intended order, Satan's plan escalates. Just like the Devil had a plan in the garden of Eden, he has a plan in the garden of America today. And the primary target of this plan is the family. As goes the family, so goes the nation.

BATTLE CRY

If Satan can dismantle God's prescribed intention and foundation of the family, it can lead to all manners of chaos, destruction, and devolution in our society. This is because the family houses the building blocks of society. It is both through and within the family that children, future leaders, and contributors of society are created and matured.

Nehemiah recognized the importance of the family; in fact, he relied on it as he fought to rebuild Jerusalem. We read that his response to the opposition carefully centered on the organization and motivation of the home. It says,

> When the Jews who lived near them came and told us ten times, "They will come up against us from every place where you may turn," then I stationed men in the lowest parts of the space behind the wall, the exposed places, and I stationed the people in families with their swords, spears and bows. When I saw their fear, I rose and spoke to the nobles, the officials and the rest of the people: "Do not be afraid of them; remember the LORD who is great and awesome, *and fight for* your brothers, your sons, your daughters, your wives and your houses." (Nehemiah 4:12–14)

Nehemiah positioned the people and proclaimed the fiercest battle cry, "Fight for your families!" Nehemiah knew that it was time for each and every person and family to defend not only the present but also the future of their people as a whole. First of all, he called the men and stationed them behind the walls. Next, he included the practical aspects of the battle; he gave every man a sword, spear, and bow. Then he brought in the spiritual portion, reminding them that it is "the Lord who is great and awesome." Finally, he compelled them with the profound call to fight for their families.

I was on a conference call not too long ago with dozens of pastors discussing, at times debating, the Christians' role as salt and light in the culture, particularly with regard to the issue of the redefinition of the family through legalizing same-sex marriage. One of the common arguments that kept resurfacing on this call was the thought that "We can't impose Christian standards on society." Yet the institution of family, and primarily of marriage, was not given to Christians only. It was given to society. It was given to the human race.

That's why John the Baptist could condemn Herod for how he was functioning in his marriage. See, Herod wasn't a believer. Didn't claim to be a believer. Didn't live as a believer. Yet John's condemnation was rooted in the fabric and function of society, not purely in religion.

Others on the call claimed that Christ never addressed the issue of homosexuality from a spiritual standpoint, biblically. I found, and still do find, it difficult to comprehend this claim in light of His clear and direct words recorded in Matthew 19. We read,

> "Have you not read that He who created them from the beginning made them *male* and *female*, and said,

'For this reason *a man* shall leave his father and mother and be joined to *his wife*, and the two shall become one flesh'? So they are no longer two, but one flesh." (vv. 4–6)

When Jesus Christ specifically referred to marriage as that between a male and a female, stating that the male and female are one in marriage, He spoke clearly and without stuttering on homosexuality, polygamy, and any other deviation from the prescribed union of marriage. Marriage is a standard not only given to Christians; it is a standard that was first established for society.

And yet once a group of people—a nation or a culture—not only allows for but also gives hearty approval to that which is in direct opposition to God's prescribed purpose and standards of the family, they reap upon themselves the main expression of His judgment. We witness this in the letter Paul wrote to the church in Rome:

For their women exchanged the natural function for that which is unnatural, and in the same way also the men abandoned the natural function of the woman and burned in their desire toward one another, men with men committing indecent acts and receiving in their own persons the due penalty of their error. (Romans 1:26–27)

When they give "hearty approval" (Romans 1:32) to those who practiced the opposition of God's standards and did not "see fit to acknowledge God any longer, God *gave them over . . ."* (Romans 1:28) to a litany of consequences creating personal, familial, and cultural chaos. It is more than fair to say that this is what we have been experiencing over the last four decades in our country as we have witnessed the dire ramifications—socially, economically, and morally—attached to the breakdown of our homes and our nation.

THE CRISIS IN OUR NATION

After more than thirty years of failed social programs and billions of governmental dollars aimed at fixing homes, communities, schools, and our country, the once stable America is on a downward spiral. Couples live as if they were wed by the Secretary of War rather than by the Justice of the Peace. We are still hearing the figure of a 50 percent failure rate for new marriages, a rise that shot up from single digits once the no-fault divorce was introduced legal on January 1, 1970. Materialism has become more important than maintaining marriages and personal happiness has taken priority over family unity.

The devaluation of women through the curse of pornography and the glorification of violence on television and in the movies have fueled family breakdown as well. Not to mention the devaluation that comes through popular music lyrics that portray women as objects to be used, whether sung by a man or a woman.

In such an environment, it is no wonder that teen pregnancy continues to skyrocket and that gangs flourish in our cities—and yes, they have moved to the suburbs too. There is no longer any such thing as fleeing the problem of our society's disintegration. Urban problems are now suburban problems in many areas.

Yet in the inner city, the breakdown of the family is the greatest. Nearly seven out of ten black children are growing up without a father. Two-parent families are now the exception in the inner city and nearing the exception in the three major culture and ethnic groups in our nation: white, Hispanic, and black (an average of 44 percent belong to single-parent families).[1]

Social science statistics objectively reveal a connection between a fatherless home (either through absence or neglect) with all of the major social ills which can plague a person. Fathers are critical to the foundation of a home. Fatherlessness leads to some of the greatest, most detrimental pathologies that afflict a nation. These pathologies unravel the fabric of stability in any land. Not only do they create chaos, but they also lay a heavy burden on the taxpayers who must foot the bill for increased welfare, crime, drug addiction, and the consequences of an illiterate and uneducated nation.

It is estimated that the decreased earnings and consequent

loss of tax revenue and economic investment of high school dropouts from one year alone will cost our nation more than $319 billion in lost wages over the lifetime of that one class.[2]

Yet what I don't want you to do is to let all of this bad news discourage you. The family is fixable. Your willingness to learn about God's kingdom agenda to be one family under God is a great step toward that end. It is my hope that God will use this book, and the Bible study we've produced to go along with it, to educate and inspire you in your walk with Him and in your family relationships.

REBUILDING ONE FAMILY UNDER GOD

As you develop in your spiritual life through our study of God's Word and apply it to the family under God, I think you will find yourself entering into a whole new realm of spiritual life and see how the kingdom perspective can make a difference both for time and eternity. The problems seem enormous, but if each of us do our part, we can—like Nehemiah, who rebuilt Jerusalem in just fifty-two days—make swift and solid strides to healthier families, stronger communities, and a better tomorrow in our land.

Thousands of years ago, Nehemiah gave us the rally cry for the rebuilding of our country and our culture, and it begins with our homes. It begins with our families. It begins with men taking responsibility within the walls of their own homes, family members accessing and using the sword of the

Spirit that is the Word of God, aligning ourselves underneath the sovereign authority and power of God, and fighting for our homes.

Friend, it is high time to fight for not only our own families but also the families of our children and our children's children.

See, Satan's goal is not merely to disrupt and destroy your family. It is to disrupt and destroy your future and the futures of your family members. He wants your children to witness things happening in your home or in the homes within our culture that will set up a negative paradigm for them once they establish their own homes. In doing so, he sets in motion a destructive, cyclical archetype for the carrying on of generational curses, chaos, and dysfunction.

Only when we return to God's design and purpose for the family will we return to God. When we return to God and align our families under Him, we will experience the peace, protection, and restoration that the Israelites knew in the days of Nehemiah.

Too many in the body of Christ today have grown complacent toward the attack on the biblical family, and the call to the preservation thereof. Too many feel that it does not relate directly to them and so they have not recognized the massive curveball being hurled by Satan that seeks to topple the future of our homes and country.

Family members, position yourselves firmly within your

own walls—shore up your own homes, making certain that you provide the healthiest environment for your own family. Then, study the sword of the Spirit that is the Word of God in order to equip you to stand against the Enemy's opposition; Satan's schemes. Know that we serve an awesome and powerful God.

And fight for your families, for their future—for the future of all.

CHAPTER TWO

THE FOUNDATION OF FAMILY

Some time ago, I noticed some fissures that had appeared on one of the inside walls of our home. It wasn't long before I called in a painter to patch them up with plaster and repaint the wall. After he had finished, everything looked good as new.

Unfortunately though, about a month later the same cracks reappeared on the wall. Except this time they had come back as a family of cracks with nieces, nephews, uncles, and cousins—smaller spider-web cracks surrounding the original. So I assumed what I needed was a different painter. Someone who really knew what he was doing this time. When I called the new painter over to fix my wall, he just stared at it for a while and then bluntly said, "I can't help you."

"Excuse me?" I replied, "Why can't you help me?"

"Because you don't have a problem with cracks on your wall."

After which I looked at the cracks on my wall. And then I looked at the crackpot standing right in front of me telling me that I don't have a problem with cracks on my wall, and then I said, "Explain those," pointing at the cracks on my wall.

"Well, sir," he began, "those are cracks on your wall. But they are not your problem. Your problem is that you have a shifting foundation. The foundation underneath your home is moving. It is faulty. The cracks on your wall are merely reflective of a deeper problem."

"I'm listening," I said, "Go on."

"If you don't solidify the foundation you will forever be performing patchwork on the walls of your home. You don't only need a painter. You first need someone to work on your foundation."

What he was saying was that if he were to repair the cracks again by plastering and painting without someone else coming in to fix the foundation, the cracks would simply reappear again, this time bringing even more of their cousins along.

"Until you fix your foundation," he said, "your war with the cracks will never end."

Scripture tells us another story about the need for a strong and solid foundation. This story is located in the kingdom book of Matthew. It is part of Jesus' greatest teaching on the kingdom, His Sermon on the Mount. In this chapter we read about two very different men who were each building a house, yet on two very different foundations.

One man built his house on the shaky and uncertain foundation of sand. The other man built his house on the solid foundation of rock. The test of these foundations showed up quickly when the storms hit. The foundation that had been built upon the sand swiftly crumbled while the house that stood on the solid foundation remained intact.

In this biblical parable, a house can refer to many things. It can refer to a person's life, church, or even our society. But it can also, quite literally, refer to a family and their home. If and when we seek to build our families on anything other than the stable foundational principles of the Word of God, it will not last when life's trials and challenges come upon us.

FAULTY FOUNDATIONS

In our society today, many of our families have a foundation problem. Because of this, the majority of them are spending their time dealing with the cracks on their walls. They are trying to plaster and patch up an argument here or a fight there or rebellious children or any number of things. They spend all of their time and money focusing on the fissures rather than solidifying the foundation. It is clear today that because of this there is family chaos in our world.

Roughly 50 percent of all marriages in America—whether

Christian or non-Christian—end in divorce. Most of the other fifty percent who stay together do so for the children, financial reasons, or convenience, not necessarily because they have a thriving, loving home.

Around thirty-five percent of all of our children today in our nation are being raised in a fatherless home. If you are an African-American, that number increases to approximately 67 percent.[3] As we are witnessing throughout our land, you can't sustain a community or a nation where the men are nowhere to be found.

We are living in a chaotic culture where even the very definition of what it means to be a family has been altered. The media has its various definitions of family. The culture has its own definitions as well. And now the government through our Supreme Court is seeking to redefine the family legally.

And this isn't merely a redefinition that seeks to present homosexual marriages equal to heterosexual marriages. Because once homosexual marriages are legalized across the board, what is to be the legal grounds to say that polygamous marriages should not be legal? Or, for that matter, incestuous marriages when a child becomes of the legal age to marry? In fact, what is to be the grounds that there should even be a legal age for marriage at all?

After all, if the argument against legalizing anything other than a heterosexual marriage primarily rests on the defense and protection of the most vulnerable citizens of all, babies and children, then in legalizing other forms of marriage there is little logical or legal argument against doing away with the age requirement for marriage. One of the great tragedies of all of this is that children will be raised to believe that this is acceptable and normal.

To clarify, marriage is not merely a Christian institution. Marriage was an institution given for the purpose, prosperity, and protection of civilization.

In fact, the disintegration of the family is the single most devastating internal issue facing our nation in general and our communities in particular.

The Brookings Institution is one of Washington, D.C.'s oldest think tanks focusing on the areas of economics, governance, and development, among other things. Brookings's findings reveal that roughly $229 billion in welfare expenses delivered from 1970 through 1996 were directly tied to the deterioration of the previously established institution of marriage, which in turn led to a dramatic increase in societal upheaval through the increase of single-parent homes, poverty, drug and alcohol abuse, domestic abuse, criminal activity, high school dropouts, and incarceration rates.[4]

Families, and the consequences attached to them, touch every area of society. To a large degree, their strengths and weaknesses determine the strengths and weaknesses of churches and communities. If there is weak male leadership in the home, the same will be true in the church. If children are rebellious in the home, the same will apply in schools and on the streets.

When a father abandons his family, a son learns that this is an option for him in the future, and a daughter learns to fear a similar desertion by the man she marries. These and far too many other situations like them are especially devastating in urban settings where, coupled with many other problems, there is a massive destruction of the family.

The cracks I experienced on the wall of my home are a perfect visual image for the condition of American society today as well. We can see "cracks" everywhere: social cracks, political cracks, moral cracks, even crack cocaine cracks.

But until we stabilize the foundation, no number of programs, government grants, or elections will be able to repair the cracks in our cultural walls. There is no place where the foundation of America needs to be stabilized more than in the home. As we saw in just one stat of many through Brookings's findings, the breakdown of the family is the single greatest contributor to the deterioration of our country.

Strong families hold the key to a strong society while, conversely, weak families lead to a weak society. This is so because every other institution in society is predicated on and dependent upon strong families. And you can't have strong families without God as their foundation.

No wonder Satan didn't bother Adam until he got married. Satan knew that in order to shut down God's program of expanding His kingdom on earth, he would have to destroy the institution at the foundation of that program—namely, the family.

As Christians, we need to make sure our families are built on the firm foundation of Christ the solid rock if we hope to help others. If our families are a mess, we don't need to be exporting that mess into the culture.

REBUILDING THE FOUNDATION ON GOD'S KINGDOM AGENDA

If America is going to rebuild its communities morally, socially, and spiritually, it is going to have to begin by rebuilding the foundations of families. If someone is building a skyscraper in the midst of a city, you can always know how high they want to go up by looking at how low they drill down. The higher the skyscraper, the deeper the pit into which to pour the foundation. You can't build a skyscraper on the foundation of a chicken coop. Neither can you build a home on one. Like sand castles on the shore of a rising tide, our families are being washed away one after another.

But we can change this. The key to transforming our society and instilling in our children hope for a brighter tomorrow comes in solidifying the family unit to reflect the values of the biblical family God intended it to be. It starts with each one of us reflecting God and His image for how He designed us and modeling that reflection within the roles of the biblical home. It starts with understanding the principles and precepts of God's kingdom, so that through them we might establish kingdom families who honor Him.

Unfortunately today, far too few people have a full understanding of God's kingdom. Let me set the stage for the remainder of our time looking at the family under God through this: If you are an American, you are most likely an American because you were born here. If you are a part of the kingdom of God, it is because you have been born again into His kingdom. The reason why you do not want to miss a full comprehension of the kingdom is not only because it affects you, but it also is the key to understanding the Bible. The unifying central theme throughout the Bible is the glory of God and the advancement of His kingdom. The conjoining thread from Genesis to Revelation—from beginning to end—is focused on one thing: God's glory through advancing God's kingdom.

When you do not have that theme, then the Bible becomes disconnected stories that are great for inspiration but seem to be unrelated in purpose and direction. The Bible exists to share God's movement in history toward the establishment and expansion of His kingdom highlighting the connectivity throughout which *is* the kingdom. Understanding that increases the relevancy of this several-thousand-year-old manuscript to your day-to-day living, because the kingdom is not only then and in the future, but it is also now.

It also shines a light of relevancy on why we are to apply

what Scripture says to the definition of the family. The closer God is to the definition of the family, the more order and productivity there is in the family. The further God is from the definition of the family, the more chaos is experienced not only in the family but everywhere else the family interacts.

Throughout the Bible, the kingdom of God is His rule, His plan, His program. God's kingdom is all-embracing. It covers everything in the universe. In fact, we can define the kingdom as God's comprehensive rule over all creation. It is the rule of God (theocracy) and not the rule of man (homocracy) that is paramount.

Now if God's kingdom is comprehensive, so is His kingdom agenda. The kingdom agenda, then, may be defined as *the visible demonstration of the comprehensive rule of God over every area of life.*

That has some serious implications for us. The reason so many of us as believers are struggling in our families is that we want God to bless our agenda for our home rather than us fulfilling His agenda. We want God to okay our plans rather than our fulfilling His plans. We want God to bring us glory instead of us bringing Him glory through the family structure as He has established it.

THE FIRST FAMILY

One of the rules of studying the Bible is called the Law of First Mention. The Law of First Mention simply states that if you want to see what God says about a matter, look at the first time He brings it up. You do this because the first time He brings it up will typically tell you how He thinks about it. Everything else will build on that first time. While it may add to it or expand it, it doesn't cancel out His first mention unless He says that it does at a later point.

The concept of family is first mentioned in the book of Genesis. Even before there was sin, there was family. The divine institution of the family was placed in a sinless environment created by God. Looking at the book of Genesis in chapter 1, we read that God has been very active creating many different things. He has created the heavens and the earth in such a way that they are functional, vibrant, and pulsating with life.

On the fifth day, God formed the creatures that would live upon the earth. Then on the sixth day, He came to the paramount of His creation purposes—the creation of mankind.

In Genesis chapter 1, we read:

> Then God said, "Let Us make man in Our image, according to Our likeness; and let them rule over the fish of the sea and over the birds of the sky and over the cattle and over all the earth, and over every creeping thing that creeps on the earth." God created man in His own image, in the image of God He created him; male and female He created them. God blessed them; and

God said to them, "Be fruitful and multiply, and fill the earth, and subdue it; and rule over the fish of the sea and over the birds of the sky and over every living thing that moves on the earth." (vv. 26–28)

A number of things come out in verse 26. First, we see the word "Us" referring to the Triune God: Father, Son, and Spirit. The Trinity consists of three individual and unique persons who make up the One unified reality of the Godhead. Secondly, we see the commission of mankind that is to bear this Trinitarian image of God. An image is simply a mirror—a reflection. God created humanity (body, soul, and spirit) to mirror Him, and then He established them in the divine institution called family to reproduce His image.

Therefore the goal of people in general, and the family in particular, is to mirror God in the visible realm predicated on His reality in the invisible. The family is to be the visible photograph of God Himself.

Simply put, the family's mission is the replication of the image of God in history and to carry out His divinely mandated dominion ("let them rule"). Personal and familial happiness is to be a benefit of a strong family, but it's not the mission. The mission is the reflection of God through the advancement of His kingdom and rule on earth. Happiness becomes the natural benefit when this goal is being actualized.

The problem today is that we have transposed the benefit with the goal, so when the benefit is not working out—happiness—we quit and move on. However, what you need to keep in mind is that happiness was never God's first concern. Rather, happiness and satisfaction are to be a natural outgrowth of fulfilling God's first concern. When we make His first concern our first concern, we will experience the benefits that come with it. But if we focus on the benefit without getting back to the purpose, we may wind up losing both the purpose and the benefit.

Family was established to provide the opportunity and framework for individuals to collectively carry out the plan of God in history. In particular, that plan includes the replication of God's image and the implementation of His kingdom rule, or *dominion*, on earth. Dominion simply means ruling on God's behalf in history so that history comes under God's authority.

THE DOMINION OF THE FAMILY

In Genesis we read about God creating man, male and female, and after doing so, He gives them a common commission, to "let them rule." A correct understanding of this passage is critical to the success of having one family under God. To gain that understanding, let's look at the historical context within which the family was first placed.

When Satan rebelled, God set forth to create the human

race in order to rule over His created order. We see this in Psalm 8:

> When I consider Your heavens, the work of Your fingers,
> The moon and the stars, which You have ordained;
> What is man that You take thought of him,
> And the son of man that You care for him?
> Yet You have made him a little lower than God,
> And You crown him with glory and majesty!
> You make him to rule over the works of Your hands;
> You have put all things under his feet. (vv. 3–6)

This is why, when God created Adam and Eve, He said, "Let them rule over the fish of the sea and over the birds of the sky and over the cattle and over all the earth" (Genesis 1:26). Then God told them to "subdue" the earth (v. 28). This is known in theological terms as the Dominion Covenant.

In other words, it was impossible that God would not have a kingdom that would rule over and defeat the kingdom of Satan. When Jesus Christ sets up His millennial kingdom, it will be the final, triumphant declaration of God's glory. Satan will then be chained up during that time to demonstrate his utter defeat and judgment (see Revelation 20:1–3).

Yet, for now, God has created you and me to harness and rule a part of His creation. Every person was created with that divine intent.

Why is it important for you to grasp the unfolding of God's kingdom? Because when God established the first family and said "let them rule," He stated that He would not rule independently of man—that mankind's decisions would now carry weight regarding what He did or did not do. And He did this for one reason—to demonstrate to the Devil that He could do more through a lesser creature in manifesting His glory than through the once shining star.

See, numbers of people think that there is a battle going on between God and the Devil. There is no battle going on between God and the Devil. If there were, it wouldn't last long. That's like saying, "Tony Evans and Mike Tyson are fighting." Sure, we might both climb into the ring together to duke it out, but I would be no match for Mike.

Satan, a created creature, is no match for the omnipotent Creator. That's not even a fight. But God created inferior creatures, humanity (Psalm 8:5), who are not even competition with Satan or his demons on our own, to demonstrate that in this spiritual battle, even the inferior creature can win when he or she operates according to God's governance, authority, and kingdom agenda. You and I were cast in a cosmic conflict to manifest God's rule in history for the advancement of His kingdom and the reflection of His glory. And one way this is done is through the Dominion Covenant—the ability of mankind to rule through decisions that are made.

Keep in mind that while God has turned over the managerial responsibility for ruling, He has not turned over absolute ownership of the earth to mankind. Yet by turning over the management of the earth to man, God has established a process, within certain boundaries, whereby He respects man's decisions—even if those decisions go against Him, or even if those decisions are not in the best interest of that which is being managed.

God said, "*Let them rule.*" While God retains absolute, sovereign authority and ownership, He has delegated relative authority to humanity within the sphere of influence that each person has been placed.

For example, the bank may own the house that you live in, but it is your responsibility to pay a monthly mortgage on the house that you say you "own," as well as to maintain it, for good or for bad. Now, anyone knows how great it feels to walk into a brand new house that you have just purchased, and think to yourself, "I own this house." But the truth is, in most cases, the bank owns that house.

The bank does not get involved with the everyday duties of running your house; that is your responsibility, but the bank owns the house. Nor does the bank force you to have a clean house or prevent you from having a junky one. That is up to you. Yet, similarly, the bank does not give up ultimate ownership of the house just because you are the one living in it and managing it. If you do not make your payments, you will be the one who faces the consequence of no longer having that house.

The same holds true in the realm where you have been assigned to rule. God is the ultimate owner. He has delegated the responsibility to manage it without having delegated His sovereignty over and within it. Your decisions directly affect the quality of life within the sphere in which you function and will have a large bearing on whether or not your realm of influence increases or decreases with time.

The tragedy for many people is that they have followed after Satan, have stopped trying to be a manager over what God has delegated, and have started trying to be an owner, thus parroting Satan's sin.

What we see in the continuation of Genesis 1:26 is God delegating to mankind the full responsibility for managing His earthly creation. God decides to indirectly control the affairs of earth by letting mankind exercise direct dominion. He has placed an agent on earth to serve as His representative to carry out His desires in history.

Not only does God proffer the delegation to rule, He also grants the freedom, responsibility, and the right to rule on His behalf as owner. But what He does not do is *force* man to rule. He says, "*Let* them rule." He does not say He is going to make them rule.

What that means is that you can have a happy family or a miserable family depending on whether or not you are exercising your rule in reflection of God's image. God isn't going to make you rule. He isn't going to make you have a productive and fulfilling home. He sets up the fundamentals of the family and gives you the option of utilizing them.

Oftentimes, the well-being of the home is determined by whether the man is reflecting God's image in his role or the woman is reflecting Him in hers. Once that mirror gets broken, the reflection that is supposed to happen in the relationship gets broken with it. Virtually every time there is a family breakdown, it is because one or both parties are functioning outside of the covenantal bonds of marriage. They are functioning with a broken mirror, and as a result, they are failing to actualize the managing rulership God has given them.

What Satan tries to get us to do is to either relinquish our management by handing it over to him through deceiving us into believing that he has authority, or he tries to get us to manage poorly based on our own judgments and distorted worldviews. It isn't until we rule with wisdom under the comprehensive rule of God that we will become the managers He intended. It is then that we enter into the complete realization of the divine design for how a healthy family is to function under God.

CHAPTER THREE

THE FOUNDATION OF SINGLEHOOD

One of the most critical aspects to building healthy families that is often overlooked in Christendom is the importance of building healthy singles. Before any family came together and was created on earth through a marriage, both Adam and Eve were single.

An area that we often fail to focus on in building strong families is in building strong singles. A strong single will contribute to a strong family. A weak single will contribute to a weak family. Before we ever get family right, we have to get singlehood right.

We have already looked at the creation account in Genesis in the last chapter, but let's review it here in connection with singlehood. The name Adam refers to is that "which comes from the ground." God made man from the very ground He had just created and the very ground Adam was appointed to oversee—the place where his managerial responsibilities were to be carried out.

To put it simply, mankind is nothing much more than dignified dirt. It's important for each of us to understand where Adam came from because it is in understanding where Adam came from that we also understand where we ultimately came from as well. Essentially, we came from the ground. When we die, we're going back to the ground. On our very best day, we are a composite of the dirt intricately formed together by our Creator God and infused with the breath of life.

In order for Adam to live as a successful single, his first frame of reference was the recognition of this reality along with the humility to live life underneath the leadership of the Lord God, which we will look at later in this chapter. As long as he kept that mindset and functioned according to that truth, he would have the tools to make productive decisions.

In addition, Eve was made from Adam's rib, a lateral position in value. And before Eve was brought to Adam, she was made for God. She was fashioned by Him and for Him and His purposes that she might also have dominion. Eve is not merely an add-on to Adam; rather, she is a fully capable woman who, in her singlehood, communed with God before ever being brought to Adam.

In fact, God's creation of Eve was not a result of a request by Adam. It wasn't Adam who told God that he needed someone. Instead, God said, "It is not good for the man to be alone" (Genesis 2:18). God saw the apparent lack Adam had on his own to fulfill the Dominion Covenant so He created a helper to complete the task. Yet before Eve ever helped Adam at all, she fulfilled her highest purpose in being a helper to God Himself. She did so by fulfilling the completion of His creation.

As a matter of speaking, Adam took no part in the creation of Eve other than taking a nap. Another thing as well with regard to Adam is that he needed to learn how to be an overseer before God brought him Eve. In other words, God gave Adam a job first.

It's clear from the order in which these events took place that God wants a husband to work and to be responsible first. Marriage won't make an irresponsible man be a responsible provider and leader. God wants the best for each of His daughters, so He had Adam practice and carry out responsibility before ever introducing Eve to him.

In addition to his responsibility, though, God also gave Adam freedom. God gave Adam instructions to enjoy all the fruit of the garden, with one exception: the fruit of the Tree of the Knowledge of Good and Evil. We read,

> The LORD God commanded the man, saying, "From any tree of the garden you may eat freely; but from the tree of the knowledge of good and evil you shall not

eat, for in the day you eat from it you will surely die."
(Genesis 2:16–17)

This, based on verses 16 and 17, reveals why so many marriages dissolve. God gave Adam work to do in the garden, and with those instructions He prepared Adam to live there before ever forming a family. Yet that conversation with Adam points us to the weakness in most homes: many husbands don't know what God has said. Or they alter what God has said when applying it to their own lives and relationships. Keep in mind, Eve was not around when God gave the instructions about the tree. She had not yet been created. And Adam did not correct her when she misspoke about what God had said with regard to eating of the fruit.

When Satan questions Eve about what God said in Genesis chapter 3, her knowledge of those words could have only come from one person: Adam. Eve often takes the entire blame in sermons and studies for both subtracting from and adding to God's Word by saying, "From the fruit of the tree which is in the middle of the garden, God has said, 'You shall not eat from it or touch it, or you will die'" (Genesis 3:3). (Eve added "or touch it," and subtracted "surely" from "you will surely die.") And while she certainly is to blame for her portion as clearly recorded by Paul when he wrote that it was Eve who was "deceived," it stands to reason that Adam had his hand in this as well.

Perhaps, even, Adam may have failed to correctly communicate God's Word to her. Unfortunately today, many men either do not know God's Word themselves or do not transfer it to their family accurately as the spiritual leader of the home.

Single men and women, if your personal foundation (humility before God, responsibility over that which He has assigned you, embracing of the role in which He has created you, and an accurate understanding of God's Word) is not solid before creating a new family through marriage and children, your family's foundation will not be solid either.

Operating in your kingdom calling as a single with a kingdom perspective under the divine rule of God is fundamental to laying a strong foundation for your family.

THE LORD GOD

In Genesis chapter 2, we see another important element of a lasting foundation—the sovereign authority of God.

> Then the LORD God formed man of dust from the ground, and breathed into his nostrils the breath of life; and man became a living being. Now the LORD God planted a garden toward the east, in Eden; and there He placed the man whom He had formed. Out of the ground the LORD God caused to grow every tree that is pleasing to the sight and good for food. (Genesis 2:7–9)

In fact, this pattern that we see present itself in these three verses continues throughout the remainder of the creation narrative:

> The LORD God took the man . . . (v. 15)
> The LORD God commanded the man . . . (v. 16)
> Then the LORD God said . . . (v. 18)
> The LORD God formed . . . (v. 19)
> So the LORD God caused . . . (v. 21)
> The LORD God fashioned . . . (v. 22)

The primary element that everything else in a kingdom rests upon is the authority of the ruler. Without the proper establishment of and adherence to a ruler, anarchism ensues. This is why it is critical that we recognize that every reference to God in the Scripture with regard to God's relationship to mankind, prior to Satan's conversation with Eve, is "LORD God."

Why is this important? Because the word LORD (in all capital letters) references the name of God, which is *Yahweh*. *Yahweh* literally translates into "master, and absolute ruler."[5] When God introduces Himself to Adam relationally in the garden, and when He introduces Himself to us through Scripture with regard to His relationship to mankind, He uses the term LORD God. In all other references in these chapters that are not linked with man, God refers to Himself as *Elohim*, meaning Creator.

Clearly God is establishing the absolute and authoritative nature of His relationship with mankind through the revelation of His character and name. In fact, we know this is His objective because it is the first thing that Satan sought to undo when speaking with Eve later on in chapter 3 of Genesis.

Satan did not refer to God as *Yahweh* (LORD God). He removed the name "LORD" (master, absolute ruler) and said, "Indeed, has *God* said . . . ?" (Genesis 3:1) Satan sought to strip God of His place as absolute ruler and authority by stripping Him of His name that connoted His position. As a result, he kept the idea of religion (God) while eliminating the order of his relational authority (under God).

Religion without a relationship with God as absolute ruler and authority is no threat to Satan. Life *with* God is much different than life *under* God. In fact, Satan often uses organized religion to keep people from the one, true God. Ritual that is not predicated on an authoritative nature of relationship between God and mankind is simply legalism and is the fastest track away from God's purposes of dominion (see Eve's deception in Genesis 3).

Before any family was established, authority was established. In fact, in the very midst of forming the foundation of the family, God reinforced that foundation as being the only rightful authority.

WAITING ON GOD

If you are a Christian single, I want to encourage you to focus on the Lord rather than try and look for a mate. Let the Lord do your looking for you. A lot of singles are frustrated because they can't find Mr. or Miss Right. So they look and say, "Yeah, that's him," or "She's the one," but then it doesn't work out and they are frustrated.

But if you will stop looking and start living out your purpose under God, when the divine "Mate-Finder" is ready He will lead you to a mate, and you won't be frustrated. If you are single, the Bible urges you to keep your "antenna" tuned toward the Lord and wait for His signal. When your antenna is tuned toward the Lord, you don't need to call a dating service or make the rounds at the clubs to meet people.

This is the beauty of the book of Ruth. Ruth was not an Israelite, but she went back to Bethlehem with Naomi, even though Naomi practically guaranteed Ruth that she would never find a husband in Israel.

But Ruth went to Bethlehem seeking God, not seeking a husband. She dedicated herself to God's agenda even if it meant she would never marry (Ruth 1:16–17). And in the course of the story, God brought Boaz into her life. Ruth didn't have to go after Boaz, because God put the interest in Boaz's heart first. Then Boaz sought out Ruth.

So here was a Moabite widow who found a mate and wound up in the messianic lineage of Jesus Christ (Matthew

1:5). Ruth was looking for the Lord, and He knew where Boaz was.

Singles, it is better to wait longer for the right person than to be stuck with the wrong person. Marriage is a big enough challenge even when you find the right person. You don't need the headache and heartache of a bad relationship or an unhealthy marriage.

There's nothing wrong with marriage, emotions, or finances, but they are short-term in comparison to the kingdom. A person who is waiting for the Lord can't afford to keep his or her eyes on these things too much. This person must keep his or her kingdom perspective sharp.

Many singles are not fulfilled because they limit their lives' agendas to marriage. If God's agenda for you right now is bigger than marriage, then marriage alone can't fulfill you. And if God hasn't given you a marriage partner yet but you decide to find one on your own, you will pay a high cost for that marriage.

A question I want you to consider if you are single is this: Why does God have you single? What is He uniquely doing in you, with you, and through you that can only be done now because when you get married you won't be able to do it?

If you can't answer that question and you're living a life of frustration, you're not on track for God's best in your life. God knows that once He gives you a mate, a distraction will come into your life and you'll never be able to return to the freedoms that come from singlehood again. God is calling on singles to use their singleness for deeper commitment to Him and greater service for Him, and through this He promises His presence at a deeper level and the abiding power of His peace.

THINKING STRAIGHT WHILE YOU WAIT

While you're waiting on the Lord, make sure that you keep your thinking straight. Paul addressed this issue in verses 26–28 of 1 Corinthians 7.

Too many singles have only one thought on their minds: *I need to get married, no matter what.* But the Bible has a different emphasis. "I think then that this is good in view of the present distress, that it is good for a man to remain as he is" (v. 26). In other words, whether you're married or single, don't let your marital status dominate your thinking and focus.

Paul said this because he knew there were bigger things at stake in the Christian life than a person's marital status. This wouldn't be such a big deal for singles today except that we are guilty as a society and as a church of making single people feel like second-class citizens.

But God doesn't make any distinction between married and single people in terms of their value in His eyes. That's clear from what Paul said in 1 Corinthians 7:27, "Are you bound to a wife? Do not seek to be released. Are you released from a wife? Do not seek a wife."

If singleness were not as perfectly acceptable to God as marriage, He would have commanded all Christians to get married, and Paul would probably have gotten married or perhaps remarried. The point is that singles are not worse off than married people.

In fact, marriage has its own set of challenges and problems. "If a virgin marries, she has not sinned. Yet such will have trouble in this life, and I am trying to spare you," Paul wrote in 1 Corinthians 7:28.

Now I know that many single Christians, especially older singles, become defensive when they hear this because they think, *Oh yes, here it comes: the old "You're better off single" speech that's supposed to make me feel better about not having anyone.*

That may be some people's reaction, but there's no denying the truth that from the standpoint of kingdom service, which was Paul's focus, singles are less encumbered than married people.

We also can't deny the truth that marriage is not an automatic fix for all the needs of single people. You may say, "But Tony, I'm lonely. I have to eat alone at night and go to bed alone. I have normal emotional longings and sexual needs that are not being fulfilled, and I'm frustrated."

Well, I've counseled many married people who are so emotionally lonely and/or sexually unsatisfied that they're thinking about bailing out on their marriages and going back to being single. *The only thing more painful than being single and miserable is being married and miserable.*

Let's get our thinking straight. Anyone who thinks marriage is the end-all and be-all of life and the answer to all of a single person's dreams and problems is in for a big letdown. Marriage is wonderful, sometimes. Someone likened it once to flies on a window screen. Some are on the outside wanting in, and others are on the inside wanting out.

There's not an honest married person who will not tell you that marriage involves adjustments and problems along with the benefits. The question is not whether marriage or singleness is better but what God's will is for each of His children in light of eternity's kingdom purposes.

CHAPTER FOUR

THE FOUNDATION
OF MARRIAGE

Many men and women tell their biggest lie on their wedding day. They stand before a minister, family, and friends to commit their lives to their partner. They say, "I promise to love, honor, and cherish you in sickness and in health, for richer or poorer, for better or worse, for as long as we both shall live." Then, before long, they are divorced or wish they were.

One woman summed up the contemporary attitude this way: "When I got married I was looking for an ideal, but marriage has become such an ordeal that I want a new deal."

In some Christian homes, battle lines are drawn. Husbands are looking at their wives and saying, "If I hadn't married you, I'd be successful and important by now." And wives are looking at their husbands and saying, "If I hadn't married you, I wouldn't be stuck at home with four kids while you're out having a good time."

Negative, selfish attitudes like those are bringing tension in many homes to an explosive level. The fact is: many people simply don't know how to be married. They have never studied God's instruction manual on marriage. The Bible provides clear guidelines for making good, stable marriages, but too many people are looking for directions in other places and ruining their marriages in the process.

Many people subscribe to the popular version of love and marriage that begins when two young people fall in love, an emotional experience identified by chills, thrills, and butterflies in their stomachs. With eyes only for each other, the infatuated pair promise undying love and rush to the altar to pronounce their vows. Unfortunately, soon after they say, "I do," they *don't* anymore. Divorce seems the only way to forge a truce.

I recently came across an interesting illustration of the way marriages deteriorate over the years. The comments are those of a husband whose wife has caught a cold during the successive years of their marriage.

Year 1: "Sugar dumpling, this cold is making you mighty uncomfortable. Won't you let your lover boy take his baby to the doctor to get rid of that nasty cough?"

Year 2: "Darling, that cold seems to be getting worse. Call Dr. Miller."

Year 3: "You'd better lie down, dear, and rest with that cold before the baby wakes up."

Year 4: "Be sensible now and take care of that cold before it gets any worse."

Year 5: "You'll be all right. Just take some aspirin. By the way, how about ironing these pants for me to wear today?"

Year 6: "Would you do something about that cough, instead of barking like a seal?"

Year 7: "Woman, do something about that cold before you give me pneumonia!"

An example like this one makes a very subtle process look obvious. As a marriage decays, our focus shifts from concern for our spouse, to mutual concern, to concern for ourselves. Whether consciously or unconsciously, both husbands and wives frequently fall prey to this phenomenon. And the process of deterioration can be alarmingly quick.

How can things fall apart a week after the honeymoon? And why do marriages break down after ten, fifteen, and even twenty-five years? The root cause is the failure to understand and act on God's design and purpose for marriage.

A healthy, giving, and functioning marriage is another critical piece of the foundation of a family. Put another way, failed marriages cannot produce the unified, enduring families needed to support our troubled society. When children grow up in loveless homes, they don't learn the crucial lessons necessary to develop good self-images now and to build strong marriages for themselves later. When children see their fathers coercing submission from their mothers through fear and intimidation, they learn a warped definition of manhood and womanhood that often results in poor behavior and communication.

In order to restore our nation, churches, and communities, we must restore our families. To do that, marriages must function as God intended. That is particularly important for Christian marriages, because the church is the most potent force for community change. If the church is to be properly equipped to bring about change in our world, it needs to be focused on building and restoring strong marriages. Christian marriages must be solid so that the family unit and thereby the church can do its job effectively.

THE BLESSING OF FAMILY

God blessed the establishment of the family. When God brought Adam and Eve together, He gave them His blessing in what He had destined them to do. Keep in mind that God never blesses just to bless. There is always a reason, a purpose, for His provision. Notice the order as we revisit the following verse relating to the blessing tied to the establishment of the family. It says,

> *God blessed* them; and God said to them, "Be fruitful and multiply, and fill the earth, and subdue it; *and rule* over the fish of the sea and over the birds of the sky and over every living thing that moves on the earth." (Genesis 1:28)

First, it would help to define a blessing. A blessing is *the capacity to experience, enjoy, and extend the goodness of God in your life.* It is never just about you. While it includes you, it is also intended to extend through you to others somehow. Too many Christians today want God to bless them without being willing for God to bless others through them.

When God established the family in the garden, He told them to be fruitful and multiply. He blessed them. Then He enabled them to extend the blessing He had given them throughout the land and to those who came after them. In addition, God also blessed them through resourcing them with what they needed to carry out the rule He had given to them. He provided for them. A blessing is when God provides all that is needed for you to accomplish all there is within your destiny.

Secondly, it is important to note that after the blessing came the instructions. God blessed but then followed that up with the commission of Adam and Eve to be fruitful and multiply and to rule over that which He had placed under them. They were to serve as co-managers, partners, over the garden that had been given to them. Each of them was to assist the other in a wedded partnership—fully developing and living out God's intended purposes for their lives.

Our marriages today are deteriorating at such a high rate, not because we no longer get along but because we have lost sight of the purpose and blessing tied to a biblical marriage. Marriage is not merely a social contract; it is a sacred covenant.

Most people today view marriage as a means of looking for love, happiness, and fulfillment. Make no mistake about it, those things are important. In fact, they are critical. They are just not the most important or the most critical. Because we have turned secondary needs into primary needs, we are having trouble finding any satisfaction at all.

It is imperative that each of us learns to view marriage and family from God's perspective. Marriage is a covenantal union designed by God in order to strengthen the capability of each partner to carry out His plan in their lives.

GOD'S DESCRIPTION OF MARRIAGE

In the book of Malachi, God is complaining against His people because they have wandered away from Him. They have taken a detour from God's intended destination for them.

One of God's complaints is found in chapter 2, verses 13 and 14. We read:

> This is another thing you do: you cover the altar of the Lord with tears, with weeping and with groaning, because He no longer regards the offering or accepts it with favor from your hand. Yet you say, "For what reason?" Because the Lord has been a witness between you and the wife of your youth, against whom you have dealt treacherously, though she is your companion and your wife *by covenant.*

This passage specifically identifies the marriage union as a "covenant" between a man and a woman only. The term "covenant" used to be regularly attached to the concept of marriage. However, the word has gotten lost in our contemporary language today even though it is the biblical description of marriage used throughout Scripture.

The problems in our homes come when we don't recognize that marriage *is* a covenant. Or when we simply don't know what a covenant entails. Because if we do not know what a covenant is, then we do not know what we are supposed to have, develop, or protect over time. It's like trying to hit a bull's-eye without a target.

A covenant is more than a formal contractual arrangement. Biblically, a covenant is a spiritual and relational bond between God and a person, or people, inclusive of certain agreements, conditions, benefits, and effects.

Whenever God wanted to formalize His relationship with His people, He established a covenant. There are a number of these agreements in Scripture such as the Abrahamic Covenant, the Mosaic Covenant, the Davidic Covenant, and the New Covenant. These are formal arrangements that are spiritually binding in a legal capacity between God and a person or people.

Marriage is another covenant that God has established. As such, the marriage covenant can never operate to its fullest potential without the ongoing involvement of God. Biblical, spiritual, and theological covenants assume God's integration into every aspect of the relationship in order for that covenant to maximize its purpose.

When the practical realities of God are dismissed from the marital covenantal relationship, it becomes an invitation to the Devil to create havoc in the home. This happens because there has been a departure from God's overarching transcendence, hierarchy, and ethics that come tied to His covenant.

TRANSCENDENCE

One of the facets of a covenant, which I just mentioned, is a big theological word called *transcendence*. Transcendence simply means that God is in charge. Covenants are both initiated and ruled by God.

Now, that might seem like an obvious statement and one that we don't need to spend too much time on, but transcendence is a key principle in the marriage covenant, as well as in laying a healthy foundation for a family. In order for a covenant to successfully function, carrying with it both the benefits and security that a covenant supplies, it has to be set up according to God's expectations and regulations.

Until we recognize the covenantal aspect of transcendence in our marriages—that God instituted marriage and is therefore in charge, meaning that His viewpoint must be our viewpoint—we will never experience the productive, purposeful, and peaceful relationship we were designed to have. We will not experience it because we will continue to look at life through the limitations of physical eyes. We will miss out on the connections made in the spiritual realm.

Marriage is a covenantal agreement created to improve the ability of each partner to carry out on earth what God has designated in heaven.

Since God is ultimately in charge of the covenant of marriage, the first place to look to gain insight into the makings of a purposeful marriage is God's perspective on marriage.

Most people learn about marriage from an illegitimate source. They learn about marriage from the television, their friends, or the home that they grew up in. If you grew up in a functioning home, then that would be fine. But many did not, so the home—along with the media and friends—often merge together to form a distorted perspective on the covenant of marriage.

The Devil is sometimes the vehicle for creating this distorted perspective thus resulting in the chaos we experience in our marriages and in our lives. I know that we fuss and sometimes fight, and we think that it is the other person who is the problem. But that's exactly what the Devil wants. He wants you to believe that it's the other person who is the problem.

He wants you to believe that because he knows that you will never fix the real problem when the person you are fighting is not the real problem. The problem is a spiritual one brought on by our own sinful flesh or by a rebellious and clever enemy of God.

A lot of the stuff that we fight about as couples has nothing to do with the stuff that we are fighting about. It has to do with the consequences of our own choices as well as the demonic realm working against us. One little thing can easily turn into a conflict that puts a couple on the path to the divorce court. And you end up wondering how one little thing could do that.

It can do that because it's not the one little thing. It is the breaking of the marriage covenant either through a lack of submission under the transcendence of God, a lack of alignment, or a breaking of the covenantal rules of love and respect.

It's like asking how one small piece of fruit in the garden of Eden could have caused so much pain. It caused so much pain for all generations to come because it wasn't just about a piece of fruit. It was about the effect: the curse, which came from the cause—disobedience to God's rule.

Couples, if we cannot grasp the seriousness of making a spiritual connection in everything that goes on in our marriages, we will continue to rant and rave about the fruit, or whatever the current issue is. We will continue to focus on the thing that is happening without realizing that we must align ourselves under the fundamentals of a covenant in order to be in a position to receive the blessings that God has promised.

HIERARCHY

A second facet of God's covenants is that they are hierarchical. To put it another way, they are administered by His representatives who function according to a chain of command. God mediates His covenants through people. A hierarchy, simply defined, is an order that runs within a particular alignment.

Like automobiles that need to be properly aligned, covenants only work when they function in God's ordained order.

The same wear and tear that shows up on tires when cars are out of alignment shows up in marriages when husbands and wives ignore this vital component of a covenant as outlined in 1 Corinthians 11. If you want to experience the provision and power of the covenant then you need to operate under the legitimate hierarchy of the covenant. In 1 Corinthians 11:3, Paul lays out this principle of God's hierarchical relationships: "But I want you to understand that Christ is the head of every man, and the man is the head of a woman, and God is the head of Christ."

No person who names the name of Jesus Christ can claim autonomy. No man may say, "Because I am a man, I can do whatever I want." No, Christ is your head, your covering. You are answerable to Him.

However, my point here is that all of us are under authority. There is even a hierarchy in function within the equality of the Trinity because Paul said, "God is the head of Christ." That's why, when Jesus was on earth, He was obedient to the Father and said He would only do the Father's will. God works through a chain of command even within Himself in order to accomplish His plan and program in history.

Why is this so crucial? Because if you rebelliously break God's chain, you automatically lose His blessing and His covering. God's covenantal blessing flows through His authorized hierarchy. If you break off and do your own thing, become your own person, then you forfeit the blessings that

God designed to flow down through His chain to you. You have rebelled against God's order.

Let me show you an example of God's hierarchical blessing. Paul wrote, "For the unbelieving husband is sanctified through his wife, and the unbelieving wife is sanctified through her believing husband; for otherwise your children are unclean, but now they are holy" (1 Corinthians 7:14).

So powerful is God's chain of command that even non-Christians who come under it experience its benefits. The unbelieving members of a family are blessed as the believing member comes under God's rule and exercises his or her biblical authority. So even non-Christians get the benefits of the covenant if the Christians who are under it are in right relationship with Him.

Now you can see why Satan wants to mess up the roles God has assigned us. Satan went to Eve in the garden, not because she was morally or intellectually weaker but to bypass and distort Adam's headship.

Eve acted independently of Adam, and Adam failed to exercise his leadership. So when Eve acted independently of her head and Adam refused to lead, the roles were reversed, and Satan won that battle. Unfortunately, he still knows how to win many battles in homes today as well by getting spouses to operate outside of the hierarchy God prescribed.

ETHICS

God's covenants are also ethically established. By ethical I mean that God's covenants have specific guidelines, or rules, that govern them. Let's go back to Genesis and the garden of Eden.

> Then the LORD God took the man and put him into the garden of Eden to cultivate it and keep it. The LORD God commanded the man, saying, "From any tree of the garden you may eat freely; but from the tree of the knowledge of good and evil you shall not eat, for in the day that you eat from it you will surely die." (2:15–17)

God gave Adam a guideline to follow. God told him, "These are the rules of My kingdom. If you are going to reign here under Me, these are the rules you must obey. If you disobey My rules, you will suffer the consequences."

God has built a cause-effect relationship into His covenant rules. If you follow His rules, you get His benefits. If you follow your way, you lose His benefits and come under His penalties. When you operate under God's covenant rules, then whatever the covenant is supposed to supply you with, it will supply.

Again, this is why Satan wanted to deceive Adam and Eve. He knew if he could lead them to violate the covenant rules, they would lose the benefits and suffer God's penalty.

God told Joshua, "Be careful to do according to all the law which Moses My servant commanded you; do not turn from it to the right or to the left, *so that* you may have success wherever you go" (Joshua 1:7).

Joshua listened to what God told him. He and his leaders did what God told them, and Israel gained the Promised Land. But in the very next book of the Bible, the book of Judges, the people failed to do what God said and suffered round after round of judgments.

What's true for a nation regarding a covenant is also true for a family. When you rebel against the covenant's regulations, you lose, because there is a cause-effect relationship. It has nothing to do with whether or not you like God's rules; it's not your kingdom. If you want to operate by your own rules then you need to go out and create your own world. But as long as you are in God's world where God has set the rules, you must abide by His rules or you become a rebel against His kingdom.

Suppose you go to the top of the Empire State Building and announce, "I don't like the rule of gravity. I'm not into gravity—never have been, never will be. Can't stand the thought of 'what goes up must come down.' So today, I am going to rebel against the law of gravity. I am serving notice that this rule isn't going to tell me what to do." So you stand on the top of the Empire State Building and do your Superman thing. You jump from the precipice and wave your fist in gravity's face.

As they sweep you off the pavement, it will become undeniably clear that whether you bought into gravity or not is irrelevant. The rule is the rule, and you will pay the price for trying to break it.

CONFLICT WITHIN A COVENANT

Maybe you are one of those people in an unhappy marriage. You may sit in a pew every Sunday morning singing that your God is so high you can't get over Him, so low you can't get under Him, and so wide you can't get around Him, but back at home you and your spouse have agreed that even God can't put your marriage back together. What a contradiction! In fact, that's more than a contradiction; it's sinful.

Given the fact that our own strength is limited, it's not hard to understand why marriages aren't surviving the pressures of the twenty-first century. But we don't have to rely on our own finite powers. With Christ as our enabler, we can do all things through Christ who strengthens us (Philippians 4:13). When Paul wrote those encouraging words to the church at Philippi, he wasn't saying that he could fly on his own power if he chose to, but he was promising that everything Christ commanded him to do, Christ would enable him to accomplish.

If I had the athletic ability of Hank Aaron, I could hit many home runs. If I had the musical ability of Mozart, I could create beautiful music. If I had the mind of Einstein,

I could solve difficult equations. In other words, if I had the ability those men had, I could do what they did. That is what Paul was saying. Christ gave Paul the ability to do everything that He commanded. Because Christ commanded that marriages be permanent, each believer has the ability to accomplish God's will for marriage. The problems and challenges that marriage involves should cause us to seek and apply the power of God, not divorce our spouses.

I enjoy a good game of basketball. In fact, I'm unstoppable . . . when I play alone. When unopposed, I can make any play and shoot any shot. One day, I had an opportunity to play "one-on-one" with the former Dallas Mavericks star forward Mark Aguirre. Suddenly, I wasn't playing as well!

My ability isn't tested when I play without opposition; the test of my ability is how good I am when the other team steps onto the court. When I went up to shoot with six feet and six inches' worth of opposition in front of me, the true measure of my ability was revealed.

So it is with marriage. Conflicts shouldn't destroy the union, they should show the power of Christ within us. Because Christ never asks us to do what He has not already given us the ability to do, marital conflict can be the area in which we show the difference Christ makes.

Family counseling that gives advice on relational techniques is good, and I recommend it when marriages have reached an impasse in communication. But in order to reverse the effects of negative consequences in your home and lives and in order to evoke a blessing in your sphere of dominion, you will need more than that. You will need to address the spiritual foundation of your family. And this spiritual foundation can only be addressed spiritually.

If you want your family to fully experience God's purpose and blessings, you must function in accordance with the covenant. You must build your home on the foundation of the covenant of God.

MODELS OF SURRENDER

Part of the problem we are dealing with today in marriages is the lack of godly examples of husbands and wives who are living out their marriage according to Scriptural principles and seeing God honor their relationship. In this no-absolutes, no-rules generation, it's getting harder and harder to find real-life examples of what God designed marriage to be.

In one sense this shouldn't surprise us because we see in Proverbs 31 that an excellent woman is rare, like a precious jewel (v. 10). And I might add that excellent *men* are just as rare, if not more rare these days. But in the context of 1 Peter 3, an excellent, or holy, woman is someone who trusts in God and is submissive to her husband, truly honoring and respecting him.

Marriage is a means to greater dominion over the life God has given you. In order to carry out the greatest influence in your life, it is important for both partners to work together.

Adam was to offer leadership through being the provider, protector, and the priest. Eve was fashioned for her own personal dominion by being a helper in the process. God said of Adam's need for a mate, "I will make him a helper suitable for him" (Genesis 2:18).

SO WHAT DOES IT MEAN TO HELP?

When some men hear the word *helper*, they think of someone who is going to cook, clean, do the laundry, and keep the kids quiet while he watches his ball game.

Television sitcoms are full of these marriage portrayals, and the programs usually get a lot of laughs. But there's nothing funny about a husband who interprets "helper" simply as a maid, cook, and babysitter. A woman doesn't have to be a wife to fulfill any of these roles. You can hire people to do these tasks.

Now don't misunderstand me, this doesn't mean a wife can neglect her responsibilities at home. There is no substitute for her touch in the home—either through carrying out the responsibilities herself or overseeing others who carry them out, but if that's all her role consists of then something is wrong because this is not the primary way that a wife serves as a helper in God's kingdom.

An unfortunate yet common belief in Christian circles is that since God deemed Eve as a "helper" for Adam that women are somehow "less valuable" than men. In fact, women are frequently compared to the Holy Spirit in His role of "Helper" —the part of the Trinity that does a substantial amount of work but gets very little recognition and appears to have the least amount of authority of the Trinity. Yet a deeper examination of the word used for "helper" in the original language is eye-opening for anyone who has never studied it before.

The Hebrew words translated "helper suitable for him" in the creation story are important to examine because they are uniquely powerful. The words are *ezer*[6] and ke*negdo*[7]. The word *ezer* occurs twenty-one times in the Old Testament, with only two of those occurrences relating to a woman. The remaining instances the word is used in refer directly to God the Father, the first member of the Trinity, in a superior form. Let's take a look at a few:

> "There is none like the God of Jeshurun,
> Who rides the heavens to your help [*ezer*] . . ."
> (Deuteronomy 33:26)

> "Our soul waits for the LORD;
> He is our help [*ezer*] and our shield." (Psalm 33:20)

> "But I am afflicted and needy;
> Hasten to me, O God!

You are my help [*ezer*] . . ." (Psalm 70:5)

"Our help [*ezer*] is in the name of the LORD . . ."
(Psalm 124:8)

The term *kenegdo* was added to *ezer* in order to distinguish it from every other time in the Old Testament that it was used to refer to a strong help from God. The addition of *kenegdo* draws from its literal definition which is, "before your face, within your view or purpose."[8] It can also be translated as "a completion of" or "counterpart to." Through a careful look at the original language, it is easy to determine that Eve's role was not one of subservience, maid service, or even that of being a slave. In the original Hebrew, hers is a strong help comparable to that of God the Father Himself.

Those who attempt to misuse Scripture by painting it as a reflection of a misogynist worldview that seeks to oppress and negate the value of women clearly have not taken an accurate look at the original language or at the context in which the Scripture was penned.

The precise terminology which God chose to use for His purpose and intention of women is identical to that which He used to refer to Himself as the primary person in the Godhead. A woman's help can only be defined as a strong help and completion.

Yet, if being a helper is a position of strength and honors

God while building up the marriage, why aren't more women doing this? Because they aren't hanging out with the holy women. Instead, they're getting their input from their unholy girlfriends, watching unholy television, listening to unholy radio, and reading unholy books. Peter said that a woman who wants to get this marriage thing right needs to be spending time in the right company.

Where is a Christian wife, particularly a young woman who is new in her marriage, going to find holy women like this? The Bible says she ought to be finding them in the church:

> Older women likewise are to be reverent in their behavior, not malicious gossips nor enslaved to much wine, teaching what is good, so that they may encourage the young women to love their husbands, to love their children, to be sensible, pure, workers at home, kind, being subject to their own husbands, so that the word of God will not be dishonored. (Titus 2:3–5)

The older women in view here are not only those further along in age, but women who are spiritually mature and able to offer a godly example. You don't go to a person who has been married for five months or married five times for advice on how to respect and submit to your husband.

What a lot of Christian wives need are godly women who

won't be telling them, "Girl, I'd leave him if I were you," or, "I wouldn't take that," when times get tough.

Of course, we're not talking about a wife enduring emotional or physical abuse from a husband who has an unhealthy view of power and control because she thinks that's what God wants her to do. It is true and unfortunate that some men in the Christian faith misuse the role of "headship" by oppressing the wife they are married to while claiming it is their biblical right as head. Bear in mind that a man is not in alignment as the head over his wife if he is not in alignment under the headship of Jesus Christ, His Word, and His principles for the role of a husband. There is no excuse for abusive behavior, and it should not be tolerated.

Titus 2:5 gives us the ultimate motivation for wives to help build godly marriages. God isn't concerned about a woman pleasing her society friends or her coworkers. His concern is the honor of His Word and the glory of His name. When marriages are out of alignment with God's will, disaster is waiting to happen. God's name is at risk of being dishonored.

WHAT DOES IT MEAN TO LEAVE, CLEAVE, AND BECOME ONE?

In Genesis chapter 2, we read:

Therefore [because she was taken out of man] shall
a man leave his father and his mother [Adam didn't

have parents but would have left them for Eve], and shall cleave unto his wife: and they shall be one flesh. (v. 24 KJV)

That verse summarizes what a marriage relationship is about: to leave, cleave, and become one. The great tragedy is that most people have heard these words many times but don't know what true oneness is.

Oneness doesn't mean sameness. Oneness means demonstrating a willingness to work together toward the same goal. Anyone working together toward the same goal will have to, out of necessity, communicate, cooperate, and merge strengths with strengths while overlooking or overcoming each other's weaknesses. This not only requires time, it requires an authentic commitment. Ladies, even if a man says that he loves you, and as much as you'd like to think that he's promising to share his whole life with you, he may be only planning to work you into his schedule. He may not be planning to cut back on any activities or give up anything for you. That kind of man doesn't know what marriage is about.

God specifically asked men to give up the closest ties we have in order to honor our wives when He said, "Therefore a man *leaves* his father and mother and *embraces* his wife" (THE MESSAGE). This is because one of a woman's greatest needs in marriage is security. That is why a woman will sometimes ask her husband to hold her. Most men misinterpret that as a request for physical intimacy, but if the emotional need for security is on her mind, she is not thinking about physical desires. Because a wife needs to feel secure, a husband must make that a priority.

He must be intentional about demonstrating to her how deep a commitment he is willing to make. When he does that, both will be able to function within the unique gifts that each possess because in security is found the freedom to fully express oneself.

Marriage is a covenantal union designed to strengthen the capability of each partner to carry out the plan of God in their lives, primarily through the institution of the biblical family. Marriage takes two individuals and makes them even stronger together as one.

CHAPTER FIVE

THE FOUNDATION OF PARENTHOOD

As a husband and father as well as a pastor, I am convinced that the responsibility of building godly homes lies at the feet of the man. This is not to discount a woman's importance and input as a parent, but God has placed men at the head of their families, and one of the primary components lacking in biblical homes today is the presence of a godly father.

What used to be considered rather unusual not too many years ago, a family without a father, is now a crisis of growing proportions. The reality in our culture today is that a staggering number of children are growing up in single-parent homes, the vast majority of which are fatherless.

The implications of this are staggering in terms of the world we have to live in and minister to. This is not theoretical for me. My church in Dallas is not immune to the problem. One Sunday morning I asked for single parents to raise their hands and then asked for those who had been raised in single-parent homes to raise their hands. In each case, more than the majority put their hands up.

Even the more liberal think tank *Child Trends*, which focuses primarily on the study of children and their development, reported findings that fly in opposition to single-parent homes or homosexual marriages. They wrote:

> Research clearly demonstrates that family structure matters for children, and the family structure that helps children the most is a family headed by two biological parents in a low-conflict marriage. Children in single-parent families, children born to unmarried mothers, and children in stepfamilies or cohabiting relationships face higher risks of poor outcomes . . . There is thus value for children in promoting strong, stable marriages between biological parents. . . . It is not simply the presence of two parents . . . but the presence of *two biological parents* that seems to support children's development.[9]

Because the absence of fathers far outweighs the absence of mothers in our nation statistically, I want to primarily address fathers and husbands in this chapter on how to stabilize their own homes on the foundation of God's Word. Ladies, keep in mind that the principles will apply—in a large part—to both parents, although the language will focus more on the father.

It used to be a lot simpler than it is today. At one time our culture shared a basic understanding about what it meant to be a father and a husband. But the role of the man has been radically redefined, leaving behind a whole generation of boys and men who aren't clear about what it means to be a man, let alone how to go about leading a home. This results in a generation of girls or women who aren't clear about what to look for in a man and who also have limited options for a healthy marriage.

PASSING ON THE FAITH

Let me give you my thesis right up front so you can see how crucial the man's role in the home is to the survival of a culture. The Bible teaches that the man's primary role in a family is to oversee the generational expansion of the Christian faith.

That is, a man is to supervise, manage, and oversee his home in such a way that a vital faith is instilled in his children and they grow up to live as followers of Jesus Christ and establish vital Christian homes in their generation.

This is no small task in itself. But it is even more far-reaching than you think because the degree to which men, and parents in general, succeed or fail in this task directly correlates with the deterioration of a family's community to which they belong.

We witness this principle underscored in Exodus 20:4–6, the second of the Ten Commandments:

> You shall not make for yourself an idol, or any likeness of what is in heaven above or on the earth beneath or in the water under the earth. You shall not worship them or serve them; for I, the LORD your God, am a jealous God, visiting the iniquity of the fathers on the children, on the third and the fourth generations of those who hate Me, but showing lovingkindness to thousands, to those who love Me and keep My commandments.

God says that the decisions of a father, and parents, have generational repercussions. What they do or don't do not only impacts their own lives, it spills over to their children and their children's children and their children's children's children.

Now that's a sobering thought. It would not be so bad if my mess stopped with me. But my mess gets passed on and on and on. And with each succeeding generation, it gets passed on worse.

Why? Because God is doing the passing on, not just the man. God is "visiting the iniquity of the fathers on the . . . third and the fourth generations."

Can you see why Satan targets parents? It's because he understands this generational relationship and principle between a father and a mother and their family. So Satan knows that if he can destroy dads or moms, he can control the generations.

This is exactly what we are seeing today in our country. We are seeing what happens when men are extricated from their roles, responsibilities, and presence in the home. We're seeing what the Devil can do if he can remove a man from the home—or even worse, keep him from ever entering the home.

Today we are seeing the frightful answer to the questions: "What would it be like to have a whole generation of children grow up never having known the love, the guidance, or the blessing of a father? What would it be like to experience a generation of children who have had no father to input values and right principles into their lives?"

It is not so much that this is a lost generation. It is more accurate to say this is the product of a lost generation. This is a fatherless generation, and I hate to imagine what our future as a nation will be like if things don't change.

The violence and destruction we are witnessing today are the negative operation of this generational principle. The good news from Exodus 20:6 is that this principle works in the positive too. Fathers, and parents, can turn this thing around for their families and ultimately for our culture.

But there is only one way to start fixing the mess we are in. We must raise up a new generation of godly men and women who will accept the challenge of reversing the trend. God says it can only be done by "those who love [Him] and keep [His] commandments" (v. 6).

To our forefathers, faith was an experience. To our fathers, faith was an inheritance. For many of us today, faith is a convenience. And if we are not careful in passing on a vital, first-hand faith to our children, faith may become a nuisance.

It is through God's faithful ones that His presence is seen and experienced in a culture. God has given the men and women of this culture a lead role in transferring the Christian faith.

A POSITIVE EXAMPLE OF PARENTHOOD

This is illustrated poignantly in Genesis 18. In this chapter, we read about the imminent judgment of Sodom and Gomorrah. When we examine this text, we see the contrast of the two men at the heart of that drama.

The first man was Lot. You recall that God was willing to spare Sodom if just ten righteous people could be found. Lot had more than half that number in his family alone, but they couldn't get ten godly people together because Lot had failed to pass the faith to the next generation. Because he failed, the culture could not be salvaged.

Standing in brilliant contrast to Lot was Abraham. Look

at what God said to Abraham in Genesis 18 in relation to His decision to judge Sodom:

> The LORD said, "Shall I hide from Abraham what I am about to do, since Abraham will surely become a great and mighty nation, and in him all the nations of the earth will be blessed? For I have chosen him, so that he may command his children and his household after him to keep the way of the LORD by doing righteousness and justice, so that the LORD may bring upon Abraham what He has spoken about him." (vv. 17–19)

It was too late for Sodom and Gomorrah, but it was not too late for everybody else because one man—Abraham—was willing to transfer his faith to his posterity.

And this wasn't a private deal either. Through Abraham's faithfulness, "all the nations of the earth" would share in the blessing. What does it take to transfer the faith across the generations so that a nation is transformed? There are at least four things involved in this transfer.

A SENSE OF DESTINY

The first thing that is involved in faith transference is a sense of destiny. You can see Abraham's destiny in the verses we just quoted from Genesis 18. He was a man chosen of God to establish a godly heritage.

Some men will say, "Well, that was Abraham. God spoke to him and made several great nations out of him. That isn't going to happen to me." Maybe not, but God wants to use you to build a great family and help build a great church that shapes a great community. That ought to be destiny enough for any Christian man.

What's missing in so many people's lives today is a sense of destiny, this conviction that they're going somewhere and that they're part of something bigger than a career. If you are going nowhere, you are going to take those who are following you with you so that they go nowhere too.

As someone has said, a person who aims at nothing will hit it every time. Our culture doesn't know where it's going. It doesn't need Christians who don't know where they're going either.

What answer would you get if you asked the average Christian, "Where are you going?" Some might say heaven, but beyond that many may not know what to say at all. They might talk about their jobs or something else by which people often define themselves, but you're not likely to hear a clear, strong statement of spiritual destiny.

Yet if the only place a person is going is to work, they are really going nowhere in terms of what we're talking about. If all someone can see in the future is the next promotion, the bigger house, or the nicer car, then they have little to pass on to the next generation.

What we offer our children and grandchildren has to be made of something other than metal, paper, or bricks. It has to have the stuff that life is made of.

One of our problems is we have aimed too low. For many of us, our ancestors looked forward to the day when their children and grandchildren would be able to pursue their dreams and live in economic stability and freedom. Many gave their lives for that day. But many of their children now live bound to a credit card. They have no sense of destiny.

The great families that helped to build America were those in which great-grandfather had a vision a century or more ago and passed it down so that today, his great-grandchildren are carrying it out in some fashion. The vision shaped the whole family.

The basic idea is that way back there, the great-granddaddy had a vision, and he never let his children get away from it. God said of Abraham, "I have chosen him, so that he may command his children and his household after him to keep the way of the LORD" (Genesis 18:19).

If there is no call of God on your life, there is no sense of destiny. Destiny always involves two things. First, there's a sense of calling, the conviction that God has you here for a special purpose. Secondly, there is a sense of vision, a dream big enough to get you where you believe God wants you to go. It involves a hope that your future is going to be better than your past and where you are going is bigger than where you have been.

A visionless father has nothing to transfer. His wife is often confused and frustrated because she doesn't quite know where things are going either as she seeks to follow his lead. And the children who are following don't know where things are headed at all so they meander through life with no sense of urgency or purpose.

What Satan did to Adam was mess up his ability to perceive his destiny. He got Adam and Eve focused on a single fruit tree when they should have been running the whole show and managing the environment. Satan got them all distracted by a piece of fruit, and they lost their mandate to subdue and rule the culture.

When Christian men and women understand that God has called them to transfer the faith to the next generation, a lot of other things fall into place. Now that doesn't mean it will be easy. The culture will still try to set the agenda for our families. But if we can go out as parents chosen and called by God and ready to fulfill His destiny for us, we can lead our families and help to recapture our culture for Christ.

A COMMITMENT TO DISCIPLINE

The second thing a man must have is a commitment to discipline. See, the only way to get from where you are to the destiny ahead of you is to discipline yourself to go there. God chose Abraham "that he may command his children and his household after him to keep the way of the LORD." Abraham was to put in place a structure whereby God's commands would be known and obeyed in his family.

Like destiny, discipline involves two things. The first is instruction. These are the biblical rules we are going to follow as a family, the things we need to know. For us as parents, this means sitting down with our children and spending the time necessary to impart the teaching they need to know to carry out the destiny God has for this family.

That is why the Bible says to train up a child in the way he should go so that later on, the instruction will hold him and guide him (Proverbs 22:6). It takes discipline to fulfill a destiny and reach a goal, and we as parents must give our families the tools they need to be successful for God.

The second thing involved in discipline is correction. The priest Eli and his household were judged by God "because his sons brought a curse on themselves and he did not rebuke them" (1 Samuel 3:13). Eli and both of his sons died because the boys turned left and Eli merely scolded them.

Kids will stray from the path because they're sinners too and because they're free moral agents who can make their own choices. The problem in our culture is not that the world's kids are all little demons while ours are all little angels. All kids are born in sin.

The problem that is helping to destroy America is that in

too many homes, there is no correction when the kids go left. Either the parents don't really believe in correction, which is the modern mindset, or more frequently there is no father around to correct the wrong and apply loving discipline.

Even if he is in the home, he often leaves the child-rearing to his wife. So mom gets to do double duty and is soon over-whelmed. The result is a generation of children who have not been corrected at home. And if they are not corrected at home, that means society must try to correct them when it's late and they're too far gone.

My father was big on correction. In fact, my times of correction at his hands were known as "sessions." My mom could correct me all day long, but I did not want a session.

I will never forget the day I got suspended from junior high school for fighting. A guy was messing with my lunch. Sticks and stones may break my bones, but don't mess with my food (it was probably fried chicken). Anyway, he and I got it on. I mean, tables were turning and chairs were flying.

I got called to the principal's office and was suspended. The principal said, "I am going to call your daddy." Lord have mercy; talk about prayer in school! I could stand anything except for that phrase, "I am going to call your daddy."

My daddy worked as a stevedore, a longshoreman, un-loading and loading ships. He was paid by the hour, and he only worked when the ships came in. So for him to come to my school, he had to punch out at work, which meant that money needed for the family was no longer available for the time he had to leave work.

You get the picture. My father was not happy when he got to school. He sat down in the principal's office while the principal explained what had happened and said I was being suspended for three days.

My father just sat there. After a few moments of silence, he looked at the principal and said, "Thank you. I promise you that Tony will never be suspended from school again." I knew what that meant!

When I got home my mother said, "Your daddy said to go down to the basement and wait for him." My father had this thing where he made you wait and think about what you had done. He would go walking up and down the hall, messing with my mind.

But finally he came down with his barber's razor strap, one of those things with two layers, and we had a "session." He said to me, "Son, are you going to get suspended for fighting again?"

"No, Dad! Jesus is my witness. No, never again!" Between licks he would ask me the same question, until he was convinced that I was never going to get suspended for fighting again.

Guess what? I never got suspended again because my father loved me enough to correct me. We have a generation of children who have never known what it is to have a man who loves them enough to correct them in love, to say to them, "You don't talk like that in this house. You don't do that in this family. You don't treat your mother or your sisters that way."

HEATHER HAS BOTH
A MOMMY AND A DADDY

It is clear that both parents are needed in raising healthy children who will one day be able to be contributing citizens in society. In fact, in an amicus brief recently submitted to the Supreme Court, as they readied themselves to hear arguments as to why homosexual marriages should be legalized, respected political scientists Harvey Mansfield (Professor, Harvard) and Leon Kass (Professor, University of Chicago) made this statement. Their words were penned with regard to their desire to urge the Supreme Court to seek a scientifically and data-driven answer to this question of homosexual marriage and as to how we can best protect our most vulnerable citizens, our children. They wrote, "Claims that science provides support for constitutionalizing a right to same-sex marriage must necessarily rest on ideology. Ideology may be pervasive in the social sciences, especially when controversial policy issues are at stake, but ideology is not science."[10]

Science and statistics clearly document the dangers to innocent and unprotected babies and children who are raised outside of a healthy home comprised of two biological parents. It is time we started listening to what history has already demonstrated rather than responding to the emotionalism of media, and propaganda tactics boldly declaring a "new normal" and that *Heather Has Two Mommies*.[11] According to God's agenda and His correct view of normalcy, Heather has both a mommy and a daddy.

An objective cry must ring out for both the permanence and exclusivity of marriage and parenting as God intended. Women were not created to be good fathers. Men were not created to be good mothers. It takes both to raise a highly dependent human being into a productive contributor within society. Both the future and success of a civilization depends on the mental, social, and developmental health of its citizens.

When a number of personal actions affect public well-being (such as running red lights, speeding, breaking and entering, and indecent exposure), we would most definitely hear an outcry against removing the legal protection for the innocent from the dangers that would come from violating these standards.

And yet when it comes to protecting the parental structure which is demonstrably healthiest and safest for our most needy, dependent, and innocent human beings—our children —we hear precious few voices who will speak up for them. Our children deserve an outcry when both the social and political sciences entirely support that their well-being is intimately tied to the foundation of the home in which they are raised.

CHAPTER SIX

THE FOUNDATION OF LEGACY

When God wanted to build His own nation and raise up a legacy of people who were holy and set apart for Him, He started this through the divine institution of the family. He chose Abraham, along with Abraham's wife, Sarah, as the vessel through which to create an entire nation. In fact, God's intentions for leaving the lasting legacy of blessing the entire world came through Abraham and the seed of his family. We review in Genesis 18:

> The LORD said, "Shall I hide from Abraham what I am about to do, since Abraham will surely become a great and mighty nation, and in him all the nations of the earth will be blessed? For I have chosen him, so that he may command his children and his household after

him to keep the way of the Lord by doing righteous-
ness and justice; so that the Lord may bring upon
Abraham what He has spoken about him." (vv. 17–19)

God validated the importance of leaving a legacy through
family to Abraham when He said that His promises to him
related to nation-building were directly tied to Abraham's
influence on his own children. Abraham's greatness as the
father of a nation didn't simply come by virtue of who he was.
God instructed Abraham to train his children, along with his
entire household, to live their lives under God. In essence,
God asked Abraham to live like Joshua, "As for me *and my
house*, we will serve the Lord" (Joshua 24:15).

God so values the family that He would consistently remind His nation that it was built on family. When He would
speak about His plan in history, He would often communicate
it in terms of family. He would refer to Himself in familial legacy descriptions such as, "I am . . . the God of Abraham, the
God of Isaac, and the God of Jacob" (Exodus 3:6).

When God sought to begin the expansion of the legacy
of His kingdom in the New Testament through the church,
He would regularly speak of it with family terminology as
well, such as "household of faith," "brothers," "sisters," etc.
The family motif for the advancement of His kingdom is all
throughout Scripture. Only as we further the foundation of
the family can we see the expansion of God's kingdom in

the world as it was designed to be.

My fellow father let me ask you: Who wakes up your family for worship on Sunday morning in your home? Who says, "It's time for us to go to church"? Who leads the way in prayers at home? Who is the first one to open the Word at your house? If it is not you, you need to start discipling your family in order to bring about a lasting legacy of faith through the lineage that God has provided for you.

Discipleship is what a man needs to fulfill his role in the family and pass the faith to the next generation, leaving a legacy. Mothers need to do this as well, but it is typically less likely that mothers need to be encouraged to do this. Unfortunately, in my experience of counseling families over three decades, it is usually the father who has dropped this ball.

Discipleship is the process of training your family to keep the way of the Lord. It includes the process of bringing your family members from spiritual infancy to spiritual maturity so that they can replicate the process with someone else.

In fact, one of the primary ways that you assure a family legacy is through a commitment to discipleship.

EVANGELIZING

Of course this starts by evangelizing your family. You are responsible to introduce your family to the Lord. Look at Genesis 17:26–27: "In the very same day Abraham was circumcised, and Ishmael his son. All the men of his household, who were born in the house or bought with money from a foreigner, were circumcised with him."

In other words, if you were going to live in Abraham's house, you were going to be circumcised. What is circumcision? It was a sign of the covenant. It was bringing the family into the faith. It was letting them know that in this house, we are committed to the Lord.

Discipleship not only means introducing your family to the faith, but developing them in the faith. That's what Ephesians 6:4 says: "Fathers . . . bring [your children] up in the discipline and instruction of the Lord."

Notice that Paul did not say mothers. Why? Because a mother's job is to help the father raise their children in the Lord, not to replace the father. A mother is to be in partnership with the father as Dad provides spiritual, financial, and emotional leadership in the home.

When I was growing up, not going to church was unheard of. Sometimes, because my father had to work some Sundays, I had to walk the five miles. I could not say, "Dad, because you are not here to drive me today, I'm not going to church." It was understood, if you lived in the Evans house, you were going to church, even if you had to walk.

Parents, if you don't have a sense of destiny, a commitment to discipline, and a design for discipleship, you don't really know what a family under God is about.

ABRAHAM'S INSTRUCTIONS

In Genesis 18:19, God gave Abraham sound, clear instruction on how to construct a family that would leave a lasting legacy.

One of the things that Abraham was to do was to give his family a sense of destiny, a sense of purpose that grew out of knowing his own purpose. Our world is full of meaningless distraction but very little purpose, and purposeless parents raise purposeless children. All great people have before them a sense of destiny that transcends their own lives.

How do we instill a sense of purpose in our kids? We start by thinking of family life as a relay race. In a relay, everything depends on the baton. It doesn't matter how fast you run, how fine your form, or the distance between you and the runners behind you. If you fail to pass the baton, you are disqualified.

In the race of faith, the same is true. You may have fine form in the church. You may be sprinting with this committee or that. Perhaps you're rounding the track as a deacon. Great, but remember, God is the judge of this race; He's holding us accountable for making sure that our children take firm hold of the baton of faith and keep running.

PASSING THE BATON

My youngest son, Jonathan, used to lead a prayer meeting for some of his friends in our home. One day, after several of these prayer meetings had taken place, it occurred to me that though I'd been excited about the meetings, I had never offered my help. Consequently, I took my next opportunity to ask him: "Jonathan, suppose we took a verse of Scripture each week and worked on it together so that before your prayer meeting you could read the verse and give a word of encouragement. What do you think of that?"

Jonathan replied, "You know, Dad, I never thought about that, but it would be great!"

Now, he didn't know that what I had in mind was helping him take the next step toward becoming a preacher, which he has since grown into a young man attending seminary and speaking in front of churches and men's groups. My aim back then was to put into my son's hands the same baton which, years earlier, my father had passed on to me.

No wonder Satan works so hard to ruin families. He's trying to preempt the passing of the baton. Why settle for destroying a single life when, by corrupting a family, he can spread his poison through two, three, or even four generations?

Since it's clear that *someone* will pass a baton to our

children, don't you think we should reserve that right for ourselves and make sure that the job is done properly?

We need to see beyond our children to our grandchildren and even our great-grandchildren. We will have to begin looking at the world not simply for what it is but also for what we wish it to become. Having determined what we want to see in the future generations of our families, we can raise our children with a goal in mind rather than simply going through the motions for today.

An older man once asked me what I would like to have written on my tombstone when I die. I told him, "Tony Evans knew God and influenced the world for Him." He then said, "Now that you know what you'd like said about you when you die, you'd better begin working on it today."

I never forgot that because it gave me a sense of destiny. Even so for our children. What do you want them to look like when they are parents? You'd better start working on it now.

PSALM 128

Here's another ingredient of discipleship that I want to develop in some detail by taking you to my favorite passage in Scripture, Psalm 128:

> How blessed is everyone who fears the LORD,
> Who walks in His ways.

When you shall eat of the fruit of your hands,
You will be happy and it will be well with you.
Your wife shall be like a fruitful vine
Within your house,
Your children like olive plants
Around your table.
Behold, for thus shall the man be blessed
Who fears the LORD.

The LORD bless you from Zion,
And may you see the prosperity of Jerusalem all the
days of your life.
Indeed, may you see your children's children.
Peace be upon Israel!

The first thing the psalmist says in verses 1–2 is that nurturing the family begins with "everyone" being committed to the Lord. The place to start with fixing the family is fixing the people who live there. If the family is going to be right, then the members must have their lives centered in God. Otherwise, the mess in one member's life will rub off on the other family members.

"How blessed," how happy, is the person who fears the LORD, who takes Him seriously. It has to do with holding God in awe and reverence.

What happens when you fear God? He will take care of

your fortune: "You shall eat of the fruit of your hands" (v. 2a). He will take care of your feelings: "You will be happy" (v. 2b). And He will take care of your future: "It will be well with you" (v. 2c). What a guarantee!

God is saying, "You must be rooted in Me." Show me two people in a marriage who are rooted in God, and they have no reason for not making it. Show me two people who aren't rooted in God, and they're lucky if they do make it.

A second thing Psalm 128 tells us about nurturing is that a Christian family needs the right atmosphere. You as the man must create a healthy spiritual environment for your family. When verse 3 refers to "your wife" and "your children," it's obvious that God is focusing on the husband and father in the home.

A man is responsible for setting the tone in his family. That's why Satan is after men. He knows that if he can get men out of the picture, if he can keep them from being responsible, if he can turn them into "baby makers" rather than "children lovers," he can destroy the family, which destroys the church and ultimately destroys the culture.

The writer pictures the wife as a "fruitful vine" (v. 3). There are three things you need to know about vines. First, a vine clings. It will take hold of whatever it is attached to and cling to it. The atmosphere in a home should be such that a wife can wrap her "branches" around her husband for stability, security, and love.

Vines not only cling, but they climb. A healthy vine will spread out and take over a whole wall of a house. In other words, when a husband is providing the right kind of atmosphere, his wife can develop her strengths and abilities. She can grow, becoming a better woman than she ever was. If you have a stunted, non-growing wife, the problem could be that she doesn't have what she needs to cling to. She may not be getting the spiritual nurturing and nourishment she needs. Your wife should be able to say, "When I cling to my husband, things start growing out of my life that I didn't know were there."

The third thing you need to know about vines is that they produce clusters of grapes. Grapes start budding out everywhere. Grapes are used to make wine. A person who drinks enough wine will start becoming intoxicated. He will act different because the wine makes him feel good. Maybe you get the picture. If your wife is a clinging, climbing, and fruitful vine, you are going to become an intoxicated man! You are going to start feeling different. You are going to become a happy and fulfilled man because your wife will intoxicate you with her love. It will flow naturally.

But before any of that can happen, a vine has to have the right atmosphere to grow. Don't expect a summer wife if you bring home stormy winter weather. Don't expect a vineyard to grow if it's snowing and hailing when you come home.

You say, "How am I supposed to create this atmosphere

for my wife?" I have one simple answer: You out-serve her. It comes down to that.

That means putting her needs, concerns, and desires ahead of your own. It means instead of coming home and sitting down, waiting to be waited on like royalty, you get up and help. Whatever it takes, you communicate to your wife, "Honey, nothing is more important to me than making you happy."

When it comes to children, the psalmist changes the imagery from a vine to olive plants. Notice they are not trees yet, but plants. Olive plants take up to fifteen years to mature. They have to be nurtured. Olive oil was used for many things in that culture, but in order to get the good product there had to be a long process of nurturing.

The psalmist is saying that we must provide a nurturing environment for our children if they're going to grow up to be olive trees. The beauty of an olive tree was that when it matured, it would produce olives for many more years. That's the picture of children raised in a nurturing environment.

One of the great places to do family nurturing is "around the table" (v. 3b). Mealtimes provide many great teachable moments—but Dad has to be there around the table with the kids if those moments are going to be seized for God. The table is where the father provides leadership through teachable moments, correction, guidance, blessing, and intentional discipleship. The man who provides this kind of climate in the home will be blessed of the LORD (v. 4).

Notice the third thing the psalmist says about families. The family is maintained in the community of believers. "The LORD bless you from Zion," he writes in verse 5.

Zion was the city of God, Jerusalem. It was the place where a father would take his family to worship God. The author of Hebrews picks this up, saying, "You have come to Mount Zion and to the city of the living God" (Hebrews 12:22). The very next verse in Hebrews tells us that for us, Mount Zion is the church.

Mount Zion is the place where you meet God. The family that has God at its center and that gathers regularly with God's people to be affirmed and reaffirmed in the things of God, that family will be blessed.

Parents, if you are serious about having a long-term family, about passing on the faith to succeeding generations, then you had better be serious about leading your family in corporate worship. The reason we have so many failing families is that they're not involved in a spiritual maintenance program in the family of God, with the people of God.

Fourth and finally, the writer of Psalm 128 says that the believing family, when nurtured properly, will be powerful in its impact on society (vv. 5b–6). Notice the last phrase of the psalm: "Peace be upon Israel."

That's shalom, well-being in the community, because this family was right with God, right with each other, and right with other believers. When you get all of that lined up properly, guess what happens: you see the prosperity of the community. You see peace take over. You see a nation recover its spiritual health.

Some of us in America won't get to see our children's children because there's no peace. There's violence, corruption, and corrosion. The psalmist says, "If you want to fix the culture, then start with the house you live in."

How are we as families going to help influence the leaders of our society if we're not willing to lead and love and nurture our own spouses and children? Nurturing starts with your walk with God, then moves to your relationship with your family, then to your involvement in the church. Soon, your city is not the same. That's impact.

I haven't mentioned this yet in our time together, but I was born in urban Baltimore to a very volatile home situation. All I had ever known up until I was ten years old was chaos in my home. I was the oldest of four children and the atmosphere was volatile for all of us. My father and mother were in constant conflict, making divorce seem like the only possible outcome.

Having married young, they were still trying to figure out how to make life work. They often argued about how to handle finances, especially when there was little money to go around.

I could have ended up a casualty of a broken family, like so many of the kids around me in inner city Baltimore. But my life was forever changed the year I turned ten.

That was the year my dad turned to Jesus. He'd been invited to visit a nearby church for a special event. While there, two men asked him if he knew that he'd go to heaven when he died. He said he wasn't sure.

The men explained Christ's sacrificial and all-encompassing atonement and, for the first time, my dad understood the path to salvation. He didn't just accept God's salvation; he immediately became fired up about God and the Bible. He became an instant evangelist. Whenever my dad wasn't working, he'd take me along to pass out biblical tracts on street corners or in the local prison.

If I went downstairs to get a glass of water late at night, I'd see Dad reading the Bible or praying on his knees. He had to do that when my mom wasn't watching.

My mom didn't like my dad as a sinner, and she liked him even less as a saint. She did everything she could to make his life difficult. But my father did everything he could to show her love. When my mom would start in with him, he would stop what he was doing and start praying for her on the spot.

One night, my mom came down the stairs with tears in her eyes. My dad was reading his Bible. She told him that she could not understand how the more she rejected him and was unkind to him and tried to prove that believing in

God was wrong, the kinder he was to her and the more he invested in God's Word.

"I want what you have," she said, "because it must be real."

They got down on their knees and my dad led my mom to Christ. He led all of us kids to Him too and modeled the value of making God the central focus in all that we did.

He held weekly Bible studies at our kitchen table and instilled a love for church in his kids. On the Wednesday nights that he had to work late, I would walk five miles to our church. Dad taught me to view all of life through a spiritual lens.

If my dad had not exhibited the courage to change, my home would have become another statistic. I would have ended up a casualty, and my own four children might have ended up casualties too. It is common for children to end up as statistics when men do not accept their God-given responsibilities.

When fathers come home after a tough day at work, they should come home to serve, like my father did, teaching lessons around the dinner table and leading the family in worship and prayer.

For thirty-five years, my father had to lift heavy boxes as a longshoreman. But on Sunday mornings, even if he'd had to work all the night before, he'd wake us up. And I'd say, "But dad, I'm tired."

He'd say, "No, Tony. I'm the one who's tired. But we are going to church. Because for me and my house, we will serve the Lord."

Because of his encouragement and personal discipleship in my life, I became the first one in my family to ever graduate from high school. I was also the first one, even within my extended family, to ever go to college—let alone get a Master's degree and later a doctoral degree.

My father's influence and impact in my life gave me the foundation to start a church in my home with just ten people —albeit mostly relatives—which has now grown to nearly 10,000. The church ministry also served as the foundation for our national ministry, The Urban Alternative, which broadcasts my messages daily on nearly 1,000 radio outlets and in over a hundred countries around the world.

But none of that is about me. That's all about my father. Because when my father got saved and learned to fear God, he brought it home. When he brought it home, my mother became a fruitful vine and I became an olive plant around his table. He took us to Zion where I fell in love with the Word of God and sought to replicate that same love in my home with my own wife and children.

So now when my father, who is in his eighties, turns on the television, he can sometimes see his grandson, Anthony, Jr., singing Christian music to the glory of God. Or he can flip to another Christian channel and see his granddaughter, Priscilla Shirer, teaching women's Bible studies to women all across America. Or when he visits Dallas, he sees his granddaughter Chrystal leading a worship service at church or picks up her book on womanhood, or he sees his grandson Jonathan serving in both the local and national ministry offices and as a chaplain for the Dallas Cowboys.

This is all because when my dad got saved, he brought it home. He left a legacy at home. Then he went to Zion. And now he sees his children's children taking the kingdom and advancing it to the next generation in a legacy of faith.

RECLAIMING OUR DOMINION

Another ingredient for leaving a family legacy and passing on the faith to succeeding generations is that we need to reclaim dominion in Christ's name.

Remember, Sodom and Gomorrah were destroyed because God could not find ten righteous people. There were not enough believers to take dominion in those cities. Lot had not transferred his faith, so there was nobody there to salvage the culture.

Throughout the Old Testament, you read this phrase: "The God of Abraham, Isaac, and Jacob." That is, three generations of men with whom God was happy to identify. Why did God use these three generations of names? Because it was expected that the sons would continue what their fathers started.

It happens all the time in business: Smith and Son. It was understood that the son would continue what the father started. In this case, what the father started was the passing on of the true faith.

Some of us fathers have not been all that we should be. The good news is that God can take lemons and make lemonade. He can hit a bull's-eye with a crooked stick. You can't fix what was wrong yesterday, but you can repent, and you can do a lot about what happens today and tomorrow.

It may mean turning off the television and spending time on your knees with your spouse and your family. It may mean taking the Scriptures and sitting down with the family Sunday afternoon after church to ask, "How are we going to apply the truth we have heard to our home?"

Satan will try to thwart you and discourage you. Maybe the kids won't want to cooperate at first. You may feel like there's no use.

But if you will trust God, sooner or later the family is going to start lining up because God will honor your leadership as His representative leader in the home.

As a husband and father, you are the leader of your home. What you do—your choices, your spiritual life, and your involvement—directly affects those underneath your care.

I remember a time when I faced a big challenge in our home. My son Jonathan struggled in school due to ADD which severely hindered his ability to read early on. Jonathan is the baby of four children and by the time he had entered school, my wife, Lois, was working on her bachelor's degree as well as helping to run our national ministry, The Urban Alternative. She had expended a lot of energy already on the three older children, helping me start a church, and running a home. It didn't take too many signals for me to catch on quickly that if Jonathan was going to get the extra help he needed in his homework, it needed to be me who did it with him. I recall literally spending hours each evening sitting with Jonathan at the kitchen table, trying to help him learn how to read. Sometimes we would stay up until midnight just trying to get through his homework.

After a few years of working one-on-one with Jonathan in the evenings, God opened the door for us to enroll him in a specialized school that helped students with learning struggles like his. Between that school and his consistent time at home, Jonathan went on to score high enough on the college entry exam to accept his full football scholarship to Baylor University.

In fact, once he got into college, he completed his degree in only three and a half years. Jonathan is currently working on his Master's degree at Dallas Theological Seminary. In addition to that, he has grown into a mature husband and father, he assists me both in the church as well as in the national ministry, he is a powerful speaker, and he serves as the chaplain for the Dallas Cowboys.

The hours with Jonathan at the table paved the way for what God would later provide. I did what I could and left the rest with Him. As a father and as a parent, leading requires investing in the lives of your children while simultaneously seeking God's plan for them. Leading by faith involves doing all that you can for as long as you can within God's prescribed boundaries. It involves being attuned to God, waiting on Him to open up a new door with a new solution to meet the needs of those you have been charged with the responsibility and privilege to lead.

Yet unfortunately, today many will not experience the luxury and the privilege of having a godly father. There is a world of princes and princesses in our nation who have no one to let them know who they are and the hope of their future.

There is no one to have Bible study with them, lead them to church, correct them when they are wrong, teach them about life, and what it means to be responsible and make wise decisions. This has resulted in a form of spiritual castration for our young men and spiritual neediness for our young women. Their royalty has been ripped from them by a culture that doesn't recognize them as a prince or a princess of the King.

What our nation needs today are men and women who will step up and be surrogate parents to those who do not have any parents or who are missing a father or a mother. If that does not happen, then we will continue to face generations of men and women who do not know how to conduct themselves in the kingdom of God.

There is an interesting story told about a group of adolescent bull elephants who were in a zoo and acting unruly.

These elephants were at an age where they were experiencing periods of high hormonal levels, and that was showing up in their more aggressive behavior. Left unchecked, these adolescent bulls were on a path to becoming extremely dangerous, able to go on a rampage at any time. But what the zookeeper and the scientists chose to do in order to address the situation was to reflect the natural environment from which the elephants came.

Shortly after adolescent bulls break away from the herd in the wild and begin to wander away from what had been a strong matriarchal presence in their lives, older bulls become their mentors. As a result, the adolescent bulls submit to the presence and the power of the older bulls among them. In fact, they learn how to direct their hormonal upswings in more responsible manners that are productive to the herd rather than destructive. Scientists do not believe that it is as essential for the bulls to end up with their biological father in this situation as it is that they end up with consistent father figures who are willing to mentor them.

When the zookeeper introduced the adult bulls into the living space of the adolescents, they experienced exactly what they had anticipated. Where there had been chaos, there was now calm as the adults mentored the youth.

While elephants can't be compared to humans, the principles evident in their interactions reflect what psychologists observe in teen boys in conjunction with the success rates for mentoring programs all across the land. Mentoring is, in a large part, similar to surrogate parenting. It is essential to the development of a boy into a man and of a girl into a woman. In fact, whenever a young boy was earmarked to be a king later in life, there was much care by many people that went into training that boy on how to be a king. Yet somewhere along the line, we have come to believe that the princes in God's kingdom don't need any significant training at all. And that the princesses don't either.

With the growing absence of fathers in our land—either spiritually, physically, or emotionally—and with the increased workload on so many single mothers in our land, leading to a lack of time within the home, someone needs to step in as surrogate fathers and mothers to raise the next generation of men and women. And if we in the body of Christ don't do it, then it will be music, entertainment, or peers that continue to fill that void and drag our culture down a path of destruction.

The mission of revitalizing and transforming lives begins with investing in the individual through things like mentoring. The foundational truth—what a man thinks, he becomes—is highlighted throughout our land today through actions reflecting a worldview gone wild. To put it another way, one's behavior is controlled by one's thoughts. If one's thought life is changed, the person is changed. Changed individuals transform families, and transformed families restore communities.

At our church, we encourage mentoring in the public schools through our localized missional outreach. Our church currently reaches into more than sixty-five public schools in the Dallas/Fort Worth area, a ministry we have provided for close to thirty years. The church and school partnership initiative strengthens communities, and our nation, through seeking to correct improper responses to God's Word in the individual and in families, which is at the root cause for the dilemmas in society. This successful model has become a national initiative through our National Church Adopt-a-School Initiative where we seek to train church and lay leaders to implement the scalable model in their community so that our youth who lack proper role models in the home can have someone to show the way of godly principles. The church and school partnership model exists as a blueprint on how to apply the principles of the kingdom of God, while meeting the needs of hurting people through caring interventions underlined with the message of hope.

SATAN'S CONTINUED PURSUIT TO DISMANTLE FAMILIES

Seeking to dismantle and destroy the foundations of families is nothing new to Satan. His goal began with the first family of Adam and Eve but has since moved to all other families on the planet. In dismantling families, particularly through the breakdown of a covenantal heterosexual marriage, he seeks to thwart the expansion of God's kingdom on earth as well as the replication of God's image in history.

Satan's strategy began by coaxing mankind to willingly remove themselves from under God's rule. When Eve ate of the fruit and Adam willingly ate as well, Satan got them to operate according to their own rule and under their own authority. Adam and Eve disregarded God's authority, along with His instruction, thus inviting havoc into the home.

Yet not only did Satan get Adam and Eve to function out from under God's prescribed alignment with *Him*, he got them to function out from under God's prescribed alignment for them with each other. Eve became the leader while Adam became the passive responder, not to mention that he then proceeded to blame Eve for what was ultimately a lack of leadership on his part.

The result was that both shame and conflict entered into the marriage, and Adam and Eve's children suffered. Ultimately, sibling rivalry in the first family led to murder which then perpetuated itself in dysfunctional relationships among even more families, causing the entire human race to be destroyed, except for Noah and his family (Genesis 6). It is only in building our families on the unchanging foundation of the Word of God that we can stand strong against Satan's strategies to not only destroy our homes, but to also destroy our communities and the future of our nation.

One day when I was young, my mom told me the story

of the three little pigs. You know the story. The first two pigs built shaky houses, so the big, bad wolf was able to huff and puff and blow them down.

But the third little pig was together. He is my man. He built a sturdy house, so when his brothers came to him for protection, he invited them to sit down and enjoy the fire in his fireplace while the big, bad wolf huffed and puffed.

The wolf blew, but nothing happened. He blew again and nothing happened. He blew again and nothing happened. The difference was that the third pig built his house out of bricks.

The first pig built a house of straw. If you are trying to build your home on a good income, Satan is going to huff and puff and blow your house down.

The second pig's house was made of wood. If you are trying to build your home on success and fame, Satan is going to huff and puff and blow your house down.

But if you will build your house on the foundation of Jesus Christ, on the solid rock of God's Word, Satan can huff and puff while you and your family sit around the fireplace enjoying the blessing of God. And if enough fathers and mothers build homes like this, Satan can huff and puff on America, and she will not fall!

This is the stability and peace that God offers to those who will align their kingdom families under Him.

THE URBAN ALTERNATIVE

Dr. Tony Evans and The Urban Alternative (TUA) **equips, empowers,** and **unites** Christians to **impact** *individuals, families, churches,* and *communities* to restore hope and transform lives.

We believe the core cause of the problems we face in our personal lives, homes, churches, and societies is a spiritual one; therefore, the only way to address them is spiritually. We've tried a political, a social, an economic, and even a religious agenda. It's time for a kingdom agenda—God's visible and comprehensive rule over every area of life—because when we function as we were designed, there is a divine power that changes everything. It renews and restores as the life of Christ is made manifest within our own. As we align ourselves under Him, there is an alignment that happens from deep within—where He brings about full restoration. It is an atmosphere that revives and makes whole.

As it impacts us, it impacts others—transforming every sphere of life in which we live. When each biblical sphere of life functions in accordance with God's Word, the outcomes are evangelism, discipleship, and community impact. As we learn how to govern ourselves under God, we then transform the institutions of family, church, and society from a biblically based kingdom perspective where through Him, we are touching heaven and changing earth.

To achieve our goal we use a variety of strategies, methods, and resources for reaching and equipping as many people as possible.

BROADCAST MEDIA

Hundreds of thousands of individuals experience *The Alternative with Dr. Tony Evans* through the daily radio broadcast playing on nearly **1,000 radio outlets** and in over **130 countries**. The broadcast can also be seen on several television networks and is viewable online at TonyEvans.org.

LEADERSHIP TRAINING

The Kingdom Agenda Pastors (KAP) provides a *viable network* for *like-minded pastors* who embrace the Kingdom Agenda philosophy. Pastors have the opportunity to go deeper with

Dr. Tony Evans as they are given greater biblical knowledge, practical applications, and resources to impact individuals, families, churches, and communities. KAP welcomes *senior and associate pastors* of all churches.

The Kingdom Agenda Pastors' Summit progressively develops church leaders to meet the demands of the 21st century while maintaining the Gospel message and the strategic position of the church. The Summit introduces *intensive seminars, workshops,* and *resources,* addressing issues affecting the community, family, leadership, organizational health and more.

Pastors' Wives Ministry, founded by Dr. Lois Evans, provides *counsel, encouragement,* and *spiritual resources* for pastors' wives as they serve with their husbands in the ministry. A primary focus of the ministry is the KAP Summit that offers senior pastors' wives a safe place to *reflect, renew,* and *relax* along with training in personal development, spiritual growth, and care for their emotional and physical well-being.

COMMUNITY IMPACT

National Church Adopt-A-School Initiative (NCAASI) prepares churches across the country to impact communities by using *public schools as the primary vehicle for effecting positive social change* in urban youth and families. Leaders of churches, school districts, faith-based organizations, and other nonprofit organizations are equipped with the knowledge and tools to *forge partnerships* and build *strong social service delivery systems.* This training is based on the comprehensive church-based community impact strategy conducted by Oak Cliff Bible Fellowship. It addresses such areas as economic development, education, housing, health revitalization, family renewal, and racial reconciliation. We also assist churches in tailoring the model to meet the specific needs of their communities while simultaneously addressing the spiritual and moral frame of reference.

RESOURCE DEVELOPMENT

We are fostering lifelong learning partnerships with the people we serve by providing a variety of published materials. We offer booklets, Bible studies, books, CDs, and DVDs to strengthen people in their walk with God and ministry to others.

* * *

For more information, a catalog of Dr. Tony Evans'
ministry resources, and a complimentary copy of
Dr. Evans' devotional newsletter,
call (800) 800-3222,
or write TUA at P.O. Box 4000, Dallas TX 75208,
or log on to
TonyEvans.org.

NOTES

1. The Annie E. Casey Foundation, "Children in single-parent families by race (Percent)—2011," *Kids Count*, updated April, 2013. http://datacenter.kidscount.org/data/acrossstates/Rankings.aspx?ind=107.

2. Alliance for Excellent Education, "The High Cost of High School Dropouts: What the Nation Pays for Inadequate High Schools," 2007. www.all4ed.org/files/archive/publications/HighCost.pdf.

3. The Annie E. Casey Foundation, "Children in single-parents families."

4. While the Institute officially calls itself non-partisan, a recent article from *U.S. News* reported that from 2003 to 2010, 97.6% of Brookings's employees' political donations went to "democrats" and "liberals." (Danielle Kurtzleben, "Think Tank Employees Tend to Support Democrats," *U.S. News*, March 3, 2011. www.usnews.com/news/articles/2011/03/03/think-tank-employees-tend-to-support-democrats).

5. James Strong, *Strong's Expanded Exhaustive Concordance of the Bible* (Nashville: Thomas Nelson, 2009), s.v. "*Yahweh*."

6. Ibid., s.v. "*ezer*."

7. Ibid., s.v. "*neged*" (*kenegdo* is derived from *neged*).

8. Ibid., s.v. "*kenegdo.*"

9. Kristin Anderson Moore, Susan M. Jekielek, and Carol Emig, "Marriage from a Child's Perspective: How Does Family Structure Affect Children, and What Can We Do about It?" Child Trends Research Brief (June 2002): 1–2, 6. www.childtrends.org/wp-content/uploads/2013/03/MarriageRB602.pdf.

10. Leon R. Kass and Harvey C. Mansfield, "Brief of Leon R. Kass, Harvey C. Mansfield and the Institute for Marriage and Public Policy as *Amici Curiae* in Support of Petitioners," no. 12–144, January 29, 2013, 4. www.adfmedia.org/files/HollingsworthAmicus IMAPP.pdf.

11. Arguably the first lesbian-themed book for children, Lesléa Newman, *Heather Has Two Mommies* (New York: Alyson Books, 1994).

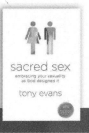

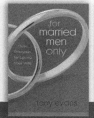